300 TRADITIONAL RECIPES GREEK COOKERY

Editions GrecoCard
ATHENS 2001
6th EDITION

- Post Cards
- Calendars
- Posters
- Playing Cards
- Maps
- Books
- Puzzles

GRECO card LTD

editorial • tourist • advertising
3 Aglavrou str. 11741 Athens
Tel.: (01) 9248292/293, Fax: (01) 9241910

Editor : George Monemvasitis
General Editing and Supervision : Si Enorasis Advertising
Recipes and Texts : Aspasia Angelikopoulu
Photography : Studio Gallegos
Colour Seperation : APOPSI
D.T.P. : ARTIA
Printing Supervision : LAITMER

Binting :T. ILIOPOULOS - P. RODOPOULOS
ISBN 960-7436-10-5

Dear friends,

This book is aimed at contemporary Greeks and foreigners who like to cook. If your family likes Greek cuisine, then you will probably be interested in trying out the 300 delicious recipes we have created with a modern approach and lots of care, and put in the cookery book you are holding in your hands. Here you will find traditional recipes which will help you enrich your knowledge of cookery and pleasantly surprise your family and friends. Among them are mair courses, desserts, holiday fare and salads, from the classic to the most innovative. In this variety we have also tried to include dishes both easy and difficult to prepare. Our intention is not to teach you old and new cookery techniques, but to help you become better and bolder in your kitchen, by suggesting deleceable new creations and broadening the skills you already have. In this book we wanted to spark off something new: fresh recipes with lots of imagination and unprecedented taste in your own kitchen. You can have fun preparing them, but you and your family can have even more fun enjoying the delicious dishes we offer you. Pick any recipe you like and don't hesitate to include it in your weekly menu.

We offer this new book on cooking and baking to contemporary readers with the certainty that it will be a most useful helper in their daily chores. So cook with love and care and earn the congratulations of your family and guests.

Wishing you every success,

The Editor

CONTENTS

OVEN TEMPERATURES

These oven temperatures are only a guide; we' ve given you the lower degree of heat. Always check the manufacturer's manual.

	C⁰ (Celsius)	F⁰(Fahrenheit)	Gas Mark
Very slow	120	250	1
Slow	150	300	2
Moderately slow	160	325	3
Moderate	180-190	350-375	4
Moderately hot	200-210	400-425	5
Hot	220-230	450-475	6
Very hot	240-250	500-525	7

APPETISERS

EGGS

SALADS

SAUCES

SOUPS

PIES

PASTA-RICE

VEGETABLES (Olive Oil - Based Recipes)

FISH - SEAFOOD

POULTRY - GAME

MEAT - MINCED MEAT

SWEETS

GREEK TRADITIONAL CHEESES

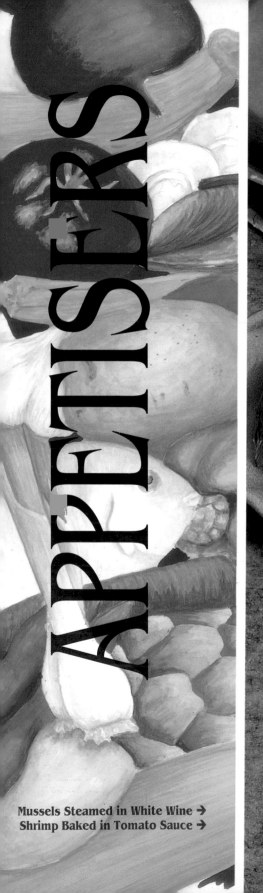

APPETISERS

Mussels Steamed in White Wine →
Shrimp Baked in Tomato Sauce →

Mussels Steamed in White Wine

SERVES 4
- 1 kg (2.2 lb) mussels
- 1 cup white unresinated wine
- 2 medium onions, finely chopped
- Salt, pepper
- 2 tablespoons parsley, finely chopped

Discard any mussels whose shells are open or broken. Clean those whose shells are closed with a stiff brush and cut off their "beards". Wash them well in running water and let them drain. Put into a pot the finely chopped onions, half the parsley, the wine and the mussels. Cover the pot tightly and boil over high heat for 6-8 minutes. Season with salt and pepper. Serve the mussels garnished with the remaining parsley.

Garides Saganaki

Shrimp Baked in Tomato Sauce

SERVES 6
- 1 kg (2.2 lb) large shrimp
- 250 gr (8.8 oz) hard feta cheese
- 1 cup olive oil
- 4 ripe tomatoes or 1 tin peeled tomatoes
- 2 medium onions, finely chopped
- 1 green pepper, finely chopped
- 1 clove of garlic, finely chopped
- 1 cup parsley, finely chopped
- Salt, pepper
- Sprinkling of paprika

Peel the tomatoes, remove the seeds and put them through a food mill. Heat the oil in a pot and sauté the onion, the garlic and the green pepper. Add the tomatoes, salt and pepper. Let the sause boil for a few minutes. Put the shrimp into an earthenware or glass baking dish and pour the sauce over them. Add the parsley, the feta broken into pieces, add a little paprika. Bake in a hot oven for half an hour.

Melitzanakia Toursi

Pickled Baby Aubergines (Eggplant)

80-90 pieces
- 2 kg (4.4 lb) baby aubergines
- 1 large bunch parsley, finely chopped
- 2 whole garlic bulbs, peeled and finely chopped
- 2 onions, finely chopped
- 2-3 carrots, grated
- 1 kg (2.2 lb) vinegar
- 1/2 kg (1.1 lb) olive oil
- 2 tablespoons salt
- Several thin stalks of celery

Wash the aubergines, cut off their stems and score them lengthwise.

Place half the salt in a pot of water, bring it to a boil, and add the aubergines. Boil them until they are tender but not too soft, then drain.

Mix together the parsley, garlic, onions and carrots. Stuff the aubergines with the mixture and carefully tie them shut with the celery stalks. Put the aubergines into a glazed earthenware container with the oil, vinegar and the rest of the salt. Leave them in a cool, dark place for 15 days.

Domatakia Toursi

Tiny Pickled Tomatoes

Approximately 20 pieces
- 1 kg (2.2 lb) tiny tomatoes
- 2 whole bulbs of garlic
- 2 cups vinegar
- Salt
- Cumin
- Red pepper

Wash the tomatoes and dry them well. Score them around the middle, put salt on the cut and let them drain. Mash the garlic to a paste and mix it with the cumin, salt and red pepper. Stuff the tomatoes with the mixture and put them in a glass or glazed earthenware jar with the vinegar and 1 1/2 cups water. Leave them in the container for 2 days.

Cheese Rolls

SERVES 5
- 300 gr (10.6 oz) phyllo dough
- 150 gr (5.3 oz) grated feta cheese
- 150 gr (5.3 oz) grated kasseri cheese
- 100 gr (3.5 oz) butter or margarine
- 1/2 cup Bechamel sauce (see Sauces)
- Pinch of nutmeg
- 2 eggs

Put the Bechamel sauce into a deep bowl and add the eggs one by one, mixing each egg in well. Add the cheeses and nutmeg and blend together thoroughly.

Cut the phyllo dough into broad strips, brush each one with melted butter and place a spoonful of the cheese mixture on each strip. Roll each one up to form a small cylinder. Put the cheese rolls on a buttered baking sheet, brush them with the rest of the butter and bake in a moderate oven for 10-15 minutes.

Bourekakia me Kima

Minced Meat Rolls

SERVES 10
- 500 gr (17.7 oz) minced meat
- 500 gr (17.7 oz) phyllo dough
- 1 large onion, finely chopped
- 2 tablespoons rusk crumbs
- Juice of 2 tomatoes
- 1 cup kefalotiri cheese, grated
- 1 cup butter or margarine
- 1 egg
- 1 bay leaf
- Salt, pepper
- Parsley, finely chopped

Sauté the onion lightly in the butter and add the minced meat. Continue to sauté, stirring continually. Add the salt, pepper, tomato juice and bay leaf. Reduce the heat and cook the meat for approximately 30 minutes longer, until all the liquid has evaporated. Add the beaten egg, the cheese, the crumbs and the parsley.

Cut the phyllo dough into strips, brush each one with butter, and place one spoonful of the mixture on each strip. Roll them up to form small cylinders, place them on a buttered baking sheet and brush them with the remaining butter. Bake in a moderate oven for 20-25 minutes.

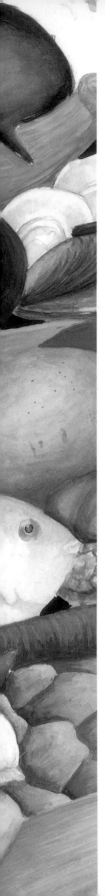

Small Cheese Pies

SERVES 8-10
- 250 gr (8.8 oz) hard feta cheese
- 10 sheets of phyllo dough
- 1 cup melted butter
- 2 eggs beaten
- A little mint, finely chopped
- Pinch of pepper

Mash the cheese with a fork and add the beaten eggs, the mint and the pepper. Cut the phyllo dough into strips 6 cm (2.4 inches) wide. Brush each strip with butter, place a teaspoonful of the filling on one end and fold it up into a triangle. Put the cheese pies onto a buttered baking sheet, brush them with a little melted butter and bake in a moderate oven 15-20 minutes until golden brown.

Cheese Patties

SERVES 8
- 250 gr (8.8 oz) kefalotiri cheese
- 2 eggs beaten
- 1/2 cup rusk crumbs
- A little parsley, finely chopped
- Pepper
- Olive oil or butter for frying

Grate the cheese coarsely. Beat the eggs well, add the rest of the ingredients except the oil, and mix together. If the mixture is not firm enough, add some more crumbs. Shape into patties and fry in oil or butter.

Salingaria Stifado

Snail and Onion Stew

SERVES 5
- I kg (2.2 lb) medium snails
- 1 kg (2.2 lb) onions, sliced and separated into rings
- 1 cup olive oil
- 2 cloves garlic, finely chopped
- 2 tablespoons vinegar
- 2 bay leaves
- A little fresh rosemary
- 5 ripe tomatoes, peeled and finely chopped
- Salt, pepper

The evening before cooking, put the snails in a bowl of water and cover it with a plate to keep them from crawling away. Wash them well, keeping only the live ones. Boil them for 15 minutes. With the point of a knife, make a hole in the rear side of each shell. Rinse them well and drain.

Heat the olive oil in a pot and brown the onions and garlic. Add the tomatoes, bay leaves, vinegar, rosemary, salt, pepper and a little water and let the sauce boil for about 15 minutes. Add the snails and continue cooking for another 20-30 minutes until most of the water has evaporated and the sauce has thickened.

Sfoungato

Eggs, Tomatoes and Courgettes, a Specialty of Crete

SERVES 4
- 500 gr (17.6 oz) courgettes (zucchini squash)
- 500 gr (17.6 oz) ripe tomatoes
- 2 medium onions, finely chopped
- 5 eggs
- 1/2 cup olive oil
- Salt, pepper

Peel the tomatoes, remove the seeds and chop them up fine. Heat the oil in a frying pan and brown the onions with the courgettes cut into round slices. Add the chopped tomatoes, salt and pepper. Cook until most of the liquid has evaporated and add the well-beaten eggs. Simmer for a few minutes. Serve hot or cold.

Spetzofai

Green Peppers and Sausages, a Specialty of Pelion

SERVES 6
- 1 kg (2.2 lb) green peppers
- 4 village-made sausages
- 1 kg tomatoes
- 2 medium onions, finely chopped
- 1 cup olive oil
- Salt, pepper
- Pinch of sugar

Put the tomatoes through a food mill. Cut the peppers and sausages into slices, heat the oil and sauté them lightly. Add the remaining ingredients and simmer until the sauce has thickened.

Dolmadakia Yalantzi

Vine Leaves Stuffed with Rice

SERVES 4
- 250 gr (8.8 oz) grapevine leaves
- 500 gr (17.6 oz) spring onions, finely chopped
- 1 cup olive oil
- 1 cup rice
- 1 small bunch dillweed, finely chopped
- 1 small bunch mint, finely chopped
- Juice of 1 lemon

Blanch the leaves, rinse with cold water and drain. Sauté the spring onions for a few minutes in half the oil. Add the rice, 1 cup hot water and the rest of the ingredients, except the oil and lemon juice. Boil the mixture for 4-5 minutes. Roll up a teaspoonful of the mixture in each leaf. Place the vine leaf rolls in a pot in firmly packed layers consisting of concentric circles. Cover them with a plate and add the rest of the oil, the lemon juice and 2 cups of water. Cook them over low heat for about half an hour, until the water has been absorbed and the rice is tender. Serve cold, garnished with lemon slices.

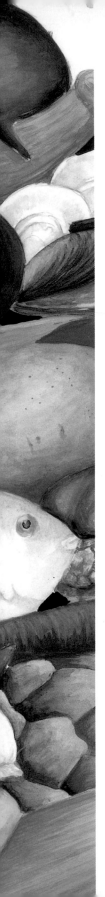

Oregano Patties

SERVES 8-10
- 1 kg (2.2 lb) potatoes
- 125 gr (4.4 oz) salted cod roe
- 1 large onion, finely chopped
- 2 eggs, beaten
- 1 level tablespoon oregano
- Crumbs of 2 rusks
- Pepper
- 1 cup flour
- Olive oil for frying

Boil the potatoes whole, remove the skins and, while still warm, put them through a food mill or purée them using a mixer. Add the remaining ingredients, except the flour and the oil. Mix well, and leave the mixture in the refrigerator until firm. Form into patties, dredge them in flour and fry them in hot oil.

Cod Roe Patties

SERVES 8
- 150 gr (5.3 oz) salted cod roe
- 200 gr (7 oz) crustless bread, soaked in water
- 3 tablespoons flour
- Half a bunch of dillweed
- Half a bunch of parsley
- A little fresh mint
- 3 spring onions
- 1 cup flour
- Olive oil for frying

Chop the herbs and onions fine. Knead them together with the bread, from which the excess water has been pressed, the roe and 3 tablespoons of flour, to form a rather firm mixture. Shape into patties, dredge them in flour and fry them in hot oil.

Kolokithokeftedes

Courgette Fritters

SERVES 8
- 1 kg (2.2 lb) courgettes (zucchini squash)
- 250 gr (8.8 oz) grated feta cheese
- 2 eggs, beaten
- 1 cup rusk crumbs
- Parsley, finely chopped
- 1 cup flour
- Salt, pepper
- Olive oil for frying

Scrape the outsides of the courgettes.Wash and grate them fine. Put them into a colander, add salt and let them drain for about an hour. Squeeze as much liquid as possible out of them. Put the courgette pulp into a bowl, add the feta cheese, eggs, crumbs, parsley and pepper, and knead the mixture. If it is not firm enough add a few more rusk crumbs or a little flour. Shape into patties, dredge them in flour and fry them in hot oil .

Revithokeftedes

Chick Pea Fritters, a Specialty of Sifnos

SERVES 6-7
- 500 gr (17.6 oz) dried chick peas
- 2 teaspoons baking soda
- 2 medium onions, finely chopped
- 1 small bunch parsley, finely chopped
- 1 egg
- 1 cup flour
- Salt, pepper
- Olive oil for frying

Soak the chick peas in warm water with the baking soda for 12-14 hours. Drain and wash them well and put them through a food mill or purée them in a mixer. Add the onions, parsley, egg, salt and pepper. Mix well and shape the mixture into patties. Dredge the patties in flour and fry them in hot oil.

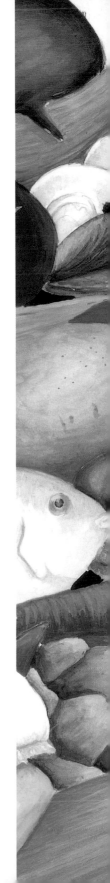

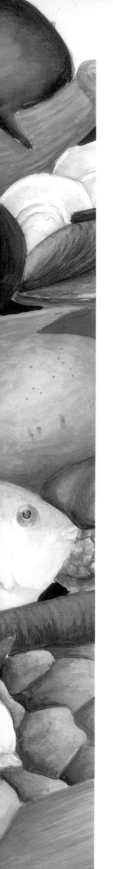

Fried Courgettes (Zucchini Squash)

SERVES 8
- 1 kg (2.2 lb) large courgettes
- 1 cup flour
- Salt, pepper
- Olive oil for frying

Wash the courgettes and cut them into thin slices. Mix the flour with the salt and pepper. Dredge the courgettes in the mixture. Heat the oil in a frying pan and fry the courgettes until golden brown. Serve at once.

Fried Aubergines (Eggplant)

SERVES 8
- 1 kg (2.2 lb) aubergines
- 1 cup flour
- Salt, pepper
- Olive oil for frying

Wash the aubergines and cut them into slices. Salt them and leave them to drain in a colander for about an hour. Rinse them and squeeze out the excess liquid. Mix the flour with the pepper. Dredge the aubergines in the flour and fry them in hot oil. Serve at once.

Fried Peppers

SERVES 6
- 500 gr (17.6 oz) sweet yellow peppers (long, tapered
type)
- Olive oil for frying
- A little vinegar
- Salt

Wash the peppers well, pat them dry and prick them with a fork. Heat the oil in a frying pan and fry the peppers, taking care they do not get too brown. Take them out of the frying pan and sprinkle with salt and vinegar.

Fried Courgettes (Zucchini Squash) ➡
Fried Aubergines (Eggplant) ➡

Kolokithoanthi Tiganiti

Fried Courgette Flowers

SERVES 5
- 15 courgette flowers
- 1/2 cup flour
- 1 egg, beaten
- 1/2 cup milk
- 1 tablespoon olive oil
- Salt
- Olive oil for frying

Wash the courgette flowers and remove the small green leaves. Make a thick batter with the flour, egg, milk, the tablespoon of olive oil and the salt.
Dip the flowers one by one into the batter and fry them in hot oil.

Kayanos

Eggs and Tomatoes, a Specialty of Laconia

SERVES 3
- 500 gr (17.6 oz) ripe tomatoes
- 6 eggs, beaten
- Salt, pepper
- 1/2 cup olive oil

Peel the tomatoes, remove the seeds and rub them through a coarse grater. Put them into a frying pan and boil until most of their juice has evaporated.
In another frying pan, heat the oil, pour in the tomatoes and sauté them for a few minutes. Add the beaten eggs, salt and pepper and stir until thick.
Variation: Just before the kayanos is done, add grated feta cheese and stir.

Pikilia Orektikon

Hors d'Oeuvres Platter

SERVES 2
- 2 slices of ham, rolled up
- 4 slices of hard salami
- 4 anchovy fillets
- A few olives, pickled in vinegar
- 1 tomato, sliced
- 2 hard boiled eggs, cut in half lengthwise
- Various pickles
- 4 radishes, peeled
- Salt, pepper
- Sprinkling of oregano

Arrange the hors d'oeuvres on a serving platter. Sprinkle salt and oregano on the tomato slices, salt and pepper on the eggs.

Gigantes Tiganiti

Fried Giant Beans

SERVES 6-7
- 500 gr (17.6 oz) giant dried white beans
- 1 cup flour
- 2 eggs
- 2 tablespoons milk
- 1 cup rusk crumbs
- Salt, pepper
- Parsley, finely chopped
- Olive oil for frying

The night before cooking, put the beans in water to soak. Next day drain them and boil them in plenty of water, until they are tender, but still firm. In one bowl, place the flour mixed with the salt and pepper, in another the beaten eggs, and in a third the rusk crumbs.

Heat the oil in a frying pan. Dip each bean first in the flour, then in the egg and finally in the rusk crumbs, before frying. Garnish with finely chopped parsley and serve at once.

Sardeles Kallonis Pastes

Salted Kalloni Sardines, a Specialty of Mytilene

- 2 kg (4.4 lb) small sardines
- Pickling salt
- Olive oil
- Vinegar

Remove the intestines from the sardines, wash and drain them well.

In a glazed earthenware or glass container, alternate layers of salt and fish, beginning and ending with a layer of salt. Put a weight on the top and let stand for a month.

Take out sardines as needed, wash them well and serve them with olive oil and vinegar.

Pickled Green Peppers

- 1 kgr. green peppers
- 2 medium onions
- 2 cups vinegar
- 1 cup water
- 1 cup rusk crumbs
- A few whole peppercorns
- 2 teaspoon salt

Wash the peppers and cut them into strips. Peel the onions, slice them and separate them into rings. Put the water, vinegar and salt into a pot to boil. Add the peppers and the onions and cook for 1-2 minutes. Turn off the heat and let cool. Fill a container with the peppers, the onions and their liquid, adding a few peppercorns. Let them stand for 10-15 days.

Pickled Red Peppers

- 2 kg (4.4 lb) red peppers
- 1 small head of cabbage
- 5 medium carrots
- 1 bunch of celery
- 1 whole bulb of garlic
- 1 tablespoon salt
- 1 kg (2.2 lb) vinegar

Shred the cabbage, carrots and celery. Add the crushed garlic and half the salt, and mix together. Wash the peppers. Cut a slit in each pepper and fill with the mixture. Put the peppers in a glass jar and cover them with the vinegar, the rest of the salt and a little water. Let them stand for 15 days.

Yoghurt, Cucumber and Garlic Dip

SERVES 6
- 2 cups strained full-fat yoghurt
- 1 medium cucumber
- 4 cloves of garlic, mashed to a paste
- 2 tablespoons olive oil
- Salt
- Pinch of pepper
- A little vinegar
- Fresh dillweed, finely chopped
- A few ripe olives

Grate the peeled cucumber on a coarse grater and press as much liquid as possible out of it. Mix the cucumber with the rest of the ingredients. Garnish with the olives.

Pickled Red Peppers ➡
Yoghurt, Cucumber and Garlic Dip ➡

Baked Giant Beans

SERVES 6
- 500 gr (17.6 oz) giant dried white beans
- 1 large onion, sliced and separated into rings
- 2-3 cloves of garlic
- 4 ripe tomatoes
- 1 scant cup olive oil
- 1 bunch parsley, finely chopped
- Salt, pepper

Put the beans in water to soak 12 hours before cooking. Drain and boil them in plenty of water. Drain again and put them in to an earthenware baking dish. Peel the tomatoes, remove the seeds, put them through a food mill and pour them into the baking dish with the beans. Add the remaining ingredients, stir and bake in a moderate oven for about one hour. If necessary, add a little water during cooking.

Tuna Salad

SERVES 4
- 1 tin of tuna
- 1 small onion, finely chopped
- Olive oil
- Lemon juice
- A little mustard
- Pinch of salt
- Parsley, finely chopped

Mix the oil, lemon juice, mustard and salt. Crush the tuna with a fork, add the onion and oil and lemon mixture and mix together. Garnish with the finely chopped parsley.

Zesty Cheese Salad, a Specialty of Macedonia

SERVES 4
- 200 gr (7 oz) feta cheese
- 1 long hot pepper
- 3-4 tablespoons olive oil
- A little vinegar

Cook the pepper under the grill. Remove the skin and seeds and cut it into small pieces. Mash the feta cheese with a fork. Put all the ingredients into the blender or blend with a mortar and pestle until they are the consistency of paste. Variation: Use soft mizithra cheese instead of feta.

Tuna salad ➡
Baked Giant Beans ➡

EGGS

Omelette

SERVES 2
- 4 eggs
- 1 tablespoon butter or margarine
- Salt, pepper

Heat the butter in a frying pan. Add the eggs, which have been beaten well with the salt and pepper. As soon as the omelette is congealed and has turned light brown on one side, turn it over and cover the frying pan with a large plate. Serve at once.

Saganaki me Tiri kai Avga

Fried Cheese and Eggs

SERVES 1
- 100 gr (3.5 oz) kefalotiri cheese
- 2 eggs
- 1 little butter
- A little flour
- Salt, pepper

Slice the cheese and dredge each slice in flour. Heat the butter in a small frying pan until very hot. Fry the cheese over medium heat. As soon as it is golden brown on one side, turn it over. Break the eggs into the pan, taking care not to break the yolks. Sprinkle with salt and pepper and let cook until set. Serve at once.

Avga me Sikotakia Poulion

Eggs with Chicken Livers

SERVES 2
- 300 gr (10.6 oz) chicken livers
- 4 tablespoons olive oil
- 2 tablespoons white unresinated wine
- 5 eggs
- Salt, pepper

Wash the livers, cut them in small pieces and let them drain. Season them with salt and pepper. Heat the oil in a frying pan and add the livers. Before they are completely cooked, add the wine and after a few minutes the beaten eggs. Let cook, stirring from time to time. Serve at once.

Avga Gemista

Devilled Eggs

SERVES 4
- 4 hard boiled eggs
- 2 tablespoons mayonnaise
- 1/2 teaspoon mustard
- 1/2 teaspoon anchovy paste
- Salt, pepper
- A few capers

Cut the eggs in lengthwise. Remove the yolks and mash them with a fork. Mix the mashed yolks with the rest of the ingredients, except the capers, and fill the halves with the mixture. Garnish with the capers.

Eggs with Feta Cheese

SERVES 2
- 4 eggs
- 1 tablespoon butter
- 150 gr (5.3 oz) feta cheese
- Salt, pepper

Heat the butter in a frying pan and add the beaten eggs, the feta, broken into small pieces and the salt and pepper. Stir constantly until the eggs are done, but do not let the cheese melt completely. Serve at once.

Avga Matia

Fried Eggs

SERVES 2
- 4 eggs
- 1 tablespoon butter or margarine
- Salt, pepper

Heat the butter or margarine in a frying pan. Break the eggs carefully into the pan, taking care they retain their shape. Season with salt and pepper. Let them cook until the whites have solidified, basting them from time to time with the butter in the pan. Serve at once.

Eggs with Cream, a Specialty of Crete

SERVES 4
- 4 tablespoons cream
- 8 eggs
- Salt, pepper

Boil the cream in a frying pan for about 6 miutes. Add the eggs, well beaten, and the salt and pepper. Stir constantly until done. Serve at once.

Avga Omeleta me Patates

Omelette with Potatoes

SERVES 4
- 6 eggs
- 4 medium potatoes
- 1 1/2 tablespoons butter or margarine
- Salt, pepper
- Olive oil for frying

Heat the oil in a frying pan. Cut the potatoes into thin slices and brown them in the oil. In another frying pan heat the butter and add the fried potatoes, the well-beaten eggs and the salt and pepper. As soon as the eggs are done on one side, turn the omelette with the help of a large plate and let it cook on the other side. Serve immediately.

SALADS

Salata me Vrasta Lahanika

Boiled Vegetable Salad

SERVES 6
- 250 gr (8.8 oz) courgettes (zucchini squash)
- 250 gr (8.8 oz) green beans
- 500 gr (17.6 oz) potatoes
- 150 gr (5.3 oz) carrots
- 250 gr (8.8 oz) beetroot
- Oil and lemon dressing
- Salt
- Parsley, finely chopped

Boil the vegetables, cut them in small pieces and salt them. Place them in layers in a salad bowl. Dress with oil and lemon and garnish with finely chopped parsley.

Patzaria Salata

Beet Salad

SERVES 6
- 1 kg (2.2 lb) beets
- Olive oil
- Vinegar
- Salt
- 2 cloves of garlic, finely chopped

Clean and wash the beets and separate the roots from the leaves. Boil the roots first, in salted water, for half an hour. Add the leaves and boil 20 minutes longer. Drain, peel the roots and cut them into slices. Place the beetroot, the leaves and the finely chopped garlic in a salad bowl and dress with oil and vinegar.
Variation: Garlic sauce (skordalia) may be used instead of oil and vinegar.

Horta Vounou Salata

Wild Greens Salad

SERVES 4
- 1 kg (2.2 lb) various wild greens
- Salt
- Oil and lemon dressing

Pick and wash the greens. Put them in a pot of boiling water and boil for about 30 minutes without covering the pot. Drain, salt and serve dressed with oil and lemon.

Kolokithakia Vrasta Salata

Boiled Courgette (Zucchini Squash) Salad

SERVES 5
- 1 kg (2.2 lb) medium courgettes
- Salt
- 6 tablespoons olive oil
- Juice of 1/2 lemon

Bring a pot of salted water to a boil and add the courgettes, which have been cleaned and washed. Boil for about 15 minutes. Slice the courgettes and pour the oil and lemon dressing over them.

Fassolia Xera Salata

White Bean Salad

SERVES 6
- 500 gr (17.6 oz) dried white
beans
- 1 medium onion, finely
chopped
- Oil and lemon dressing
- Parsley, finely chopped
- Salt

Put the beans in water to soak 12 hours before preparation time. Drain the beans, place in a pot of water and boil until tender. Drain again and put them in a salad bowl. Add salt and the chopped onion, dress with oil and lemon and garnish with finely chopped parsley.

Patatossalata

Potato Salad

SERVES 6
- 1 kg. potatoes
- 1 onion, sliced
- Juice of 1 lemon
- 1/2 cup olive oil
- Salt, pepper
- Parsley, tinely chopped
- A few ripe olives, pickled in
vinegar

Boil the potatoes whole in salted water. Peel, slice and place them in a salad bowl. Add the rest of the ingredients and srir well.
Variations: 1.The pastry may be replaced with oregano, and finely chopped pickled cucumbers added.
2.Add a little garlic, pounded to a paste. to the oil and lemon dressing.

Cauliflower Salad

SERVES 5-6
- 1 large cauliflower
- 1/2 cup olive oil
- Juice of 1 lemon
- Salt
- A little oregano (optional)

Remove any tough stems from the cauliflower and wash it. Bring a pot of salted water to a boil and add the cauliflower. Let it boil for about 25 minutes. Serve the cauliflower dressed with oil and lemon and a sprinkling of oregano.
Note: Broccoli salad may be made in the same way.

String Bean Salad

SERVES 4
- 1 kg (2.2 lb) string beans
- 6 tablespoons olive oil
- 1 tablespoon vinegar
- Salt

Clean and wash the string beans. Boil them in salted water for 20 minutes in an open pot. Dress with oil and vinegar.
Variation: The oil and vinegar may be replaced with garlic sauce (see page 48. Garlic Sauce - Skordalia).

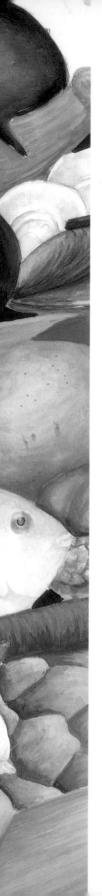

Lettuce Salad

SERVES 4
- 1 large head of lettuce
- 4-5 spring onions, finely chopped
- Salt
- Oil and vinegar dressing or oil and lemon dressing
- Fresh dill weed, finely chopped

Clean and wash the lettuce. Pat the leaves dry and cut them into thin strips. Add the onions and dillweed to the lettuce. Salt the salad and dress with oil and vinegar or oil and lemon.

Shrimp Salad

SERVES 6
- 1 kg (2.2 lb) shrimp
- 3 potatoes, boiled but not too soft
- 2 tablespoons pickled cucumbers, sliced
- 2 tablespoons capers
- Salt, pepper
- Parsley, finely chopped

For the oil and lemon dressing:
- 6 tablespoons olive oil
- Juice of 1/2 lemon
- Alittle mustrard
- Salt, pepper
- Parsley, finely chopped

Boil the shrimp in salted water, to which a little vinegar has been added. Peel and devein the shrimp, cut the potatoes into cubes, and place them in a salad bowl, along with the pickled cucumber and the capers. Stir to mix. Beat the oil and lemon dressing and pour it over the salad. Garnish with finely chopped parsley.

Lettuce Salad ➡
Shrimp Salad ➡

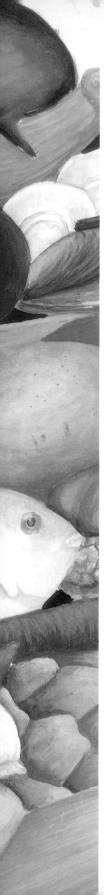

Kokino Lahano Salata

Red Cabbage Salad

SERVES 6
- 1 head red cabbage
- Oil and lemon dressing
- Salt

Shred the cabbage and wash it well. Place it in a salad bowl, add salt, and dress with oil and lemon.

Salata me Lahano kai Karota

Cabbage and Carrot Salad

- SERVES 8
- 1 small firm head of cabbage
- 3 carrots
- 1/2 cup olive oil
- Lemon juice
- Salt

Shred and salt the cabbage, and place it in a colander to wilt for 1/2 -1 hour. Rinse it well and put it in a salad bowl. Clean, wash and grate the carrots and mix them in with the cabbage. Dress the salad with oil and lemon.
Note: Prepare the oil and lemon dressing without salt, as the cabbage has already been salted.
Variation: Make the oil and lemon dressing using the juice of only 1/2 lemon and add a clove of garlic, crushed, and a little mustard.

Aubergine (Eggplant) Salad

SERVES 6
- 1 kg (2.2 lb) large purple aubergines
- 1 cup olive oil
- Juice of 1 lemon
- 2 cloves of garlic, mashed to a paste
- Salt

Prick the aubergines with a fork and bake them in the oven. Peel them and beat them in a blender with the lemon and the salt.
Continue to blend, adding the garlic and olive oil a little at a time.

Cod Roe Salad

SERVES 4- 5
- 100 gr (3.5 oz) salted cod roe
- 300 gr boiled potatoes
- 1 cup olive oil
- 1 small onion, grated
- Juice of 1 1/2 lemons

Mash the roe, potatoes and onion until smooth. Add the oil and lemon juice in turns, little by little. Garnish with olives and the heart of a lettuce or with finely chopped parsley.
Variation: Soaked and squeezed crustless bread may be substituted for the potatoes.

Garlic Sauce

- 5-6 cloves of garlic
- 150 gr (5.3 oz) boiled potatoes
- 1/2 cup olive oil
- A little vinegar
- Salt

Peel and mash the garlic to a paste. Add the potatoes and mash. Add 1-2 teaspoons vinegar and dribble in the oil, mixing constantly. Serve the skordalia garnished with olives.
Variations: 1. A little lemon may be added along with the olive oil.
2. The potatoes may be replaced with crustless bread, which has been soaked in water and squeezed.

48

Aubergine (Eggplant) Salad ➡
Cod Roe Salad ➡
Garlic Sauce ➡

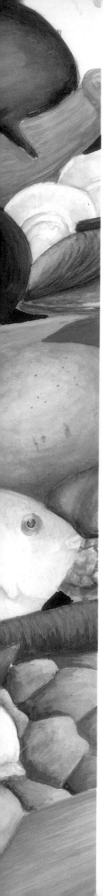

Russian Salad

SERVES 6
- 2 large carrots, boiled
- 2 large potatoes, boiled
- 1 cup peas, boiled
- 1 cup green beans, boiled
- 1 tablespoon capers
- 2-3 pickled cucumbers
- Salt, pepper
- 4 tablespoons mayonnaise (see recipe under Sauces)

To garnish:
- 2 Tablespoons mayonnaise
- Parsley leaves
- 1/2 carrot, boiled

Cut the carrots and potatoes into cubes, the green beans into small pieces and the pickled cucumber into thin slices. Put all the ingredients in a salad bowl and mix together. Spread mayonnaise over the top of the salad and garnish with parsley leaves and a few slices of boiled carrots.

Rengossalata

Smoked Herring Salad

SERVES 6
- 500 gr (17.6 oz) boiled potatoes
- 1 large onion
- 1 large carrot
- 2 smoked herring
- Oil and lemon dressing

Slice the onion thinly. Clean and grate the carrot. Cut the potatoes into cubes. Clean the herring and remove the bones, cut them in small pieces and put them in a salad bowl. Add the onion, carrot and potatoes. Mix together and dress with oil and lemon.

Beef Salad

SERVES 6

a. For the boiled beef:
- 1 kg (2.2 lb) brisket of beef
- 2 stalks celery
- A little parsley
- 1 bay leaf
- 1 onion
- 1 carrot
- Whole peppercorns
- Salt

b. For the salad:
- 3 medium potatoes, boiled and sliced
- 250 gr (8.8 oz) green beans, boiled
- 1 medium onion, sliced
- 2 medium tomatoes, sliced
- Pickled cucumbers
- Parsley, finely chopped

c. For the oil and lemon dressing:
- 1/2 cup olive oil
- Juice of 1 lemon
- 1/2 teaspoon mustard
- Salt, pepper

Bring plenty of water to a boil in a pot and add the salt and the meat, cut into serving pieces. Skim off the foam, add the remaining ingredients for the boiled beef, cover the pot and let simmer for 2 - 2 1/2 hours.

Place the salad ingredients and the meat, cut into small pieces, in a salad bowl. Beat the dressing ingredients well and pour the dressing over the salad. Stir and garnish with finely chopped parsley.

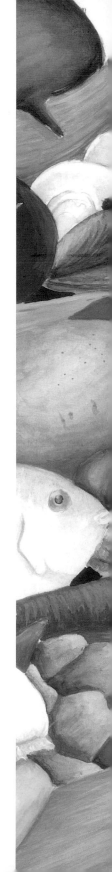

Greek Salad

SERVES 6
- 4 firm ripe tomatoes
- 1 cucumber
- 1 medium onion
- 1 green pepper
- 150 gr (5.1 oz) feta cheese
- A few ripe olives
- A few capers
- 1/2 cup olive oil
- Sprinkling of oregano
- Salt

Wash the tomatoes, peel the cucumber and cut into slices. Cut the onion and pepper in rings. Place them in a salad bowl, add the olives, capers, oregano and salt, and mix lightly. Slice the feta cheese, place it on top of the salad and dress with olive oil.

Tomato and Cucumber Salad

SERVES 4
- 1 medium cucumber
- 3 tomatoes, ripe but firm
- 5 tablespoons olive oil
- Salt
- Oregano (optional)

Wash the tomatoes and peel the cucumber, slice and place in a salad bowl. Sprinkle on the oregano and salt, and dress the salad with the olive oil.

SAUCES

Egg and Lemon Sauce

- 1- 2 cups broth from soup or liquid from entree
- 2 eggs
- Juice of 1 lemon
- A little flour

Mix the flour with the lemon juice. Beat the eggs in a bowl with the flour and lemon juice. Add the broth or other liquid little by little, beating continually. Pour the egg and lemon sauce into the pot of soup or food and stir.

Note: Remove the pot from the heat before adding the egg and lemon sauce.

Variation: If a thinner sauce is desired, you may omit the flour.

Bechamel Sauce (for Moussakas and Pastitisio)

SERVES 6
- 4 cups hot milk
- 8 tablespoons flour
- 3 tablespoons butter or margarine
- Salt, pepper
- Pinch of nutmeg

Melt the butter in a small pot, add the flour and stir well with a wooden spoon. Turn the heat down very low and add the hot milk, little by little, stirring constantly to keep the flour from forming lumps. Let the sauce thicken, stirring constantly. Add the salt, pepper and the nutmeg.

Variations: 1. When the sauce has thickened, remove it from the heat and gradually stir in two beaten eggs.

2. If the Bechamel sauce is to be used for pastitsio, stir in 1/2-1 cup grated cheese (kasseri or kefalotiri) at the end.

Saltsa Domatas me Kima

Tomato Sauce with Minced Meat

- 500 gr (17.6 oz) minced meat
- 4 ripe tomatoes or 1 tin peeled tomatoes
- 2 tablespoons butter or margarine
- 1 large onion, finely chopped
- **1 demitasse cup red wine**
- 1 bay leaf
- Parsley, finely chopped

Heat the butter in a pot and sauté the onion lightly. Add the minced meat, sauté for a few minutes longer and pour in the wine. Add the tomatoes, peeled and chopped, the bay leaf and the salt and pepper. Simmer the sauce for about 40 minutes. Ten minutes before cooking time is up, add the parsley.

Variation: Add a little stick cinnamon and 1-2 cloves to the sauce.

Saltsa Domatas

Tomato Sauce

- 2 tablespoons butter or margarine
- 1 kg (2.2 lb) ripe tomatoes
- 1 large onion, finely chopped
- Pinch of sugar
- 1 carrot, grated
- A little celery, finely chopped
- Salt, pepper

Heat the butter in a pot and sauté the onion, carrot and celery. Add the tomatoes, which have been peeled and chopped, along with the salt, pepper and sugar. Simmer the sauce for about 40 minutes. Put it through a food mill and bring it to a boil again for 2-3 minutes. The sauce accompanies pasta or rice.

Mayoneza

Mayonnaise

- 1 cup olive oil
- 2 egg yolks
- 1 tablespoon lemon juice
- 1 tablespoon vinegar
- Pinch of sugar
- 1 teaspoon mustard
- Pinch of salt
- A little white pepper

Beat the eggs, sugar, mustard, salt, pepper and vinegar. Continue to beat, adding the oil a few drops at a time. While still beating, add the lemon juice, a few drops at a time.

Saltsa Marinati gia Psaria, or Savoro

Marinade Sauce for Fish

- 2-3 cloves of garlic, finely chopped
- Rosemary
- 2/3 cup vinegar
- 1 kg (2.2 lb) ripe tomatoes
- Pinch of sugar
- Salt, pepper

Strain the oil that the fish were fried in. Heat it in a frying pan, add the flour, and brown it. Add the tomatoes, peeled and put through a food mill, the vinegar, rosemary, garlic, salt, pepper and sugar. Let the sauce boil until it is thick. Savoro can be used to marinate or accompany cold fried fish such as saddled bream, red mullet, pandora, etc.

Ladolemono

Oil and Lemon Dressing

- 1/2 cup olive oil
- Juice of 1 lemon
- Salt, pepper

Put the ingredients in a glass jar, screw on the lid and shake. This is a dressing for fish or salads.
Variations: 1. Add oregano, finely chopped parsley or finely chopped onion to the oil and lemon.
2. Add 1/2 teaspoon mustard to the oil and lemon.

58

SOUPS

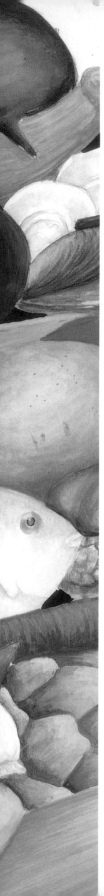

Frumenty, Sweet or Sour

SERVES 3
- 1/2 cup frumenty
- 1 tablespoon butter
- 4 cups water

Boil the water, to which the butter has been added. Add the frumenty and stir. Let it cook for about 20 minutes.

Variations: (For sour frumenty):

1. Substitute a little olive oil for the butter and add a little tomato juice and salt. Serve with grated cheese.

2. Omit the butter and one cup of the water. Add one cup of milk and some grated feta cheese. Serve the frumenty with a pat of butter melted on top.

Kakavia

Fish Soup

SERVES 6
- 1 kg (2.2 lb) various rock fish (combers, wrasses)
- 2 onions, sliced
- 2 carrots, sliced
- 1 stalk celery, finely chopped
- 3 medium tomatoes, sliced
- 1 clove garlic, crushed
- 1/2 cup olive oil
- 1 bay leaf
- Parsley, finely chopped
- Juice of 1 lemon
- Salt, pepper

Clean and wash the fish. Heat the oil in a pot and brown the onions, carrots and celery. Add the tomatoes and water and simmer for half an hour, adding a little more water if necessary. Add the fish, bay leaf, garlic, parsley, salt and pepper and continue to boil for about 20 minutes longer. Remove the heads, tails and bones from the fish and puree the soup. Serve with lemon juice and fried croutons.

Variation: Along with the fish, add various types of seafood (without the shells), i.e. shrimp, lobster, crab, mussels, etc.

Prassossoupa

Leek Soup

SERVES 4
- 500 gr (17.6 oz) leeks
- 2 carrots
- 1 bunch celery
- 1/2 cup olive oil
- Salt, pepper
- Egg and Lemon Sauce (See Sauces)

Peel and wash the vegetables. Cut the leeks and carrots into small pieces and chop the celery fine. Heat the oil in a pot, sauté the vegetables lightly, cover them with water and add the salt and pepper. Simmer until the vegetables are tender. Prepare the egg and lemon sauce and serve the soup hot.

Hortossoupa

Vegetable Soup

SERVES 5
- 3 medium potatoes
- 3 carrots
- 3 courgettes (zucchini squash)
- 1 leek
- 1 onion
- 2 ripe tomatoes
- Celery, finely chopped
- Pinch of thyme
- 1/2 cup olive oil
- Salt, pepper
- Juice of 1 lemon

Peel and wash the vegetables. Cut the potatoes, carrots and courgettes into cubes. Slice the onion and leek. Peel the tomatoes, remove the seeds and put them through a food mill. Put all the ingredients except the lemon juice in a pot, cover with plenty of water and boil for about 20 minutes. Serve the vegetable soup with lemon juice.

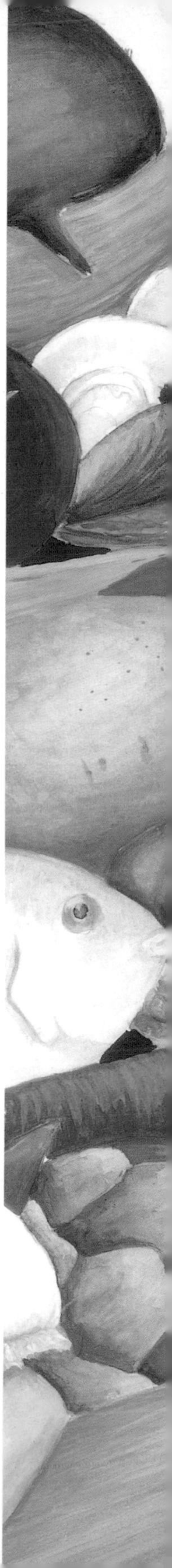

Chicken Soup with Egg and Lemon

SERVES 5
- 1 chicken
- 1 cup rice
- 1 whole onion
- Salt, pepper
- Egg and lemon sauce (see sauces)

Put the chicken into a pot and cover it with water. As soon as it begins to boil, skim off the foam and add the onion and salt and pepper. When the chicken is done, remove it from the pot along with the onion. Add the rice to the soup and let it cook. When the rice is done, prepare the egg and lemon sauce and serve the soup hot.

Onion Soup

SERVES 4
- 500 gr (17.6 oz) onions
- 1/2 cup olive oil
- 2 medium potatoes
- 1 1/4 cup tomato juice
- Salt, pepper
- Broth (optional)

Peel and wash the potatoes and cut them into cubes. Peel and slice the onions. Put the vegetables in a pot, add the tomato juice, and cover with meat broth or water. Add the salt and pepper and cook the soup over medium heat.

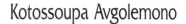

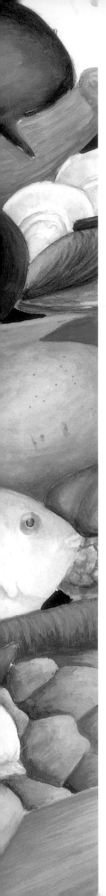

Tomato Soup

SERVES 4
- 3 ripe tomatoes
- 1/2 cup olive oil
- Salt
- 1 stalk celery
- Pinch of sugar
- 1 cup fine pasta for soup

Wash and peel the tomatoes, remove the seeds and put them through a food mill. Place them in the pot with the celery, sugar, oil, salt and plenty of water, bring to a boil and simmer for 20 minutes. Add the pasta and let the soup simmer for about 10 minutes longer. Remove the celery and serve hot.

Fassolada

White Bean Soup

SERVES 6
- 500 gr (17.6 oz) dried white beans
- 1 large onion, sliced
- 3 medium carrots, sliced
- 2 stalks celery, finely chopped
- 1 cup tomato juice
- 1 cup olive oil
- Salt, pepper

Put the beans in water to soak the evening before cooking. Next day, drain the beans, place them in a pot of water and bring to a rolling boil. Drain off the water, and put the beans back in the pot with new water and the remaining ingredients. Let the soup simmer for about an hour.

Fakes

Lentil Soup

SERVES 6
- 500 gr (17.6 oz) lentils
- 1 large onion, sliced
- 1-2 cloves garlic, sliced
- 1 bay leaf
- 1 cup tomato juice
- 1 scant cup olive oil
- Salt, pepper

Pick and wash the lentils. Place them in a pot and cover with plenty of water. When they have come to a rolling boil, drain off the water. Put them back in the pot with new water and add the remaining ingredients. Simmer the lentils for about half an hour.
Variation: The tomato juice may be omitted.

Tomato Soup ➡
White Bean Soup ➡
Lentil Soup ➡

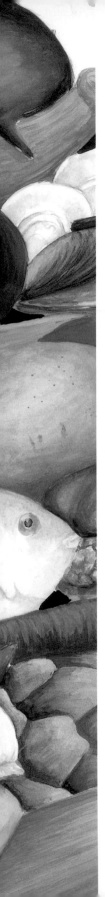

Chick-Pea Soup

SERVES 6
- 500 gr (17.6 oz) chick-peas
- 1 cup olive oil
- 3 large onion, cut into thin slices
- 1 tablespoon baking soda
- 1 tablespoon flour
- Salt, pepper
- Juice of 1 lemon

The evening before cooking, put the chick-peas in water to soak. Next day, drain them, add the baking soda, stir well and let them stand for one hour. Next wash the chick-peas thoroughly, put them in a pot and cover them with plenty of water. Bring to a boil and skim off all the scum that appears. Add the onion, salt, oil and pepper and let simmer. When the chick-peas are done, add the flour which has been mixed with the lemon juice. Bring to a boil again and serve. Variation: Add a little cumin to the soup.

Fish Soup with Egg and Lemon

SERVES 4- 5
- 1 kg (2.2 lb) fish (grouper, sea bream, sea bass)
- 3 medium potatoes
- 4 small onions
- 3 carrots
- 1 celeriac root, cut in half
- 2 medium ripe tomatoes
- 1/2 cup olive oil
- 1/2 cup demitasse cup rice
- Egg and lemon sauce (See Sauces)
- Salt, pepper

Peel and wash the vegetables and put them on to boil in a pot of water with the oil, salt and pepper. When they are almost done, add the fish, cleaned and washed, and continue boiling for 20 minutes longer. Remove the fish and vegetables and arrange them on a platter. Put the rice in the pot and boil for 15 minutes. Prepare the egg and lemon sauce and serve the soup hot.

Kreatossoupa

Meat Soup

SERVES 5
- 1 kg (2.2 lb) veal
- 1 onion
- 2- 3 stalks celery
- 2 carrots
- 1 stalk of parsley
- 1 bay leaf
- 1/2 cup tomato juice
- 1 cup rice
- Salt, pepper
- Juice of 1 lemon

Put the meat into a pot and cover it with water. When it begins to boil, skim off the foam, add the vegetables, the tomato juice, salt and pepper, and let it simmer. When the meat is tender, take it and the vegetables out of the pot. Add the rice to the bouillon and let it cook. Serve the soup with lemon juice.

Variation: The tomato juice may be omitted and the soup made with egg and lemon sause.

Youvarlakia Soupa Avgolemono

Meatball Soup with Egg and Lemon

SERVES 5
- 500 gr (17.6 oz) minced beef
- 1/2 cup olive oil
- 2/3 cup rice
- 1 egg
- 1 medium onion, finely chopped
- Parsley, finely chopped
- Salt, pepper
- Egg and lemon sauce (See Sauces)

Put all the ingredients for the meatballs except the oil into a large bowl and knead them well. Shape the mixture into small balls. Place the meatballs in a pot and cover them with water. Add the olive oil. Bring to a boil, reduce heat and simmer for about half an hour. When the meat balls are cooked prepare the egg and lemon sauce and serve hot.

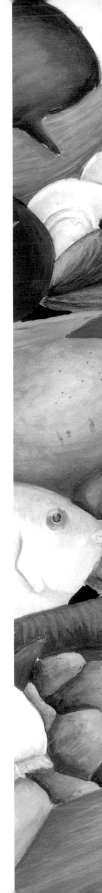

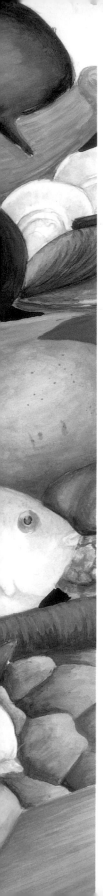

Easter Soup

SERVES 6 - 8
- 1 set lamb offal (heart, lungs, spleen, liver kidneys, a few small intestines).
- 1/2 kg (1.1 lb) spring onions, finely chopped
- 1 bunch dillweed or fennel, finely chopped
- 1 scant demitasse cup rice.
- Egg and lemon sauce (See Sauces)
- Salt, pepper
- 1/2 cup olive oil

Wash and blanch the offal. Cut it into tiny cubes. Heat the oil in a pot and sauté the offal with the onions. Add plenty of water, the dillweed, salt and pepper and let the soup simmer for about half an hour. Add the rice and boil the soup. As soon as the rice is tender, prepare and add the egg and lemon sauce.

Variation: For a lighter soup, do not sauté the offal and onions, but put all the ingredients, including the oil, on to boil at once.

Tripe Soup

SERVES 4 - 5
- Tripe of 1 sheep
- 4 cloves garlic, quartered
- 1 bay leaf
- A little rosemary
- 1/2 cup olive oil
- Salt, pepper
- Vinegar

Scrape the tripe and wash it; blanch and rinse it in cold water. Cut the tripe into thin strips. Place them in a pot with the other ingredients, cover with water, bring to a boil, and simmer for about half an hour. Serve with vinegar.

Easter Soup ➡
Tripe Soup ➡

Courgette (Zucchini Squash) Pie →
Cheese Pie →
Spinach Pie →

Dough for Pie Crust

- 500 gr (17.6 oz) flour
- 1 demitasse cup olive oil
- 1 cup lukewarm water
- 1 level teaspoon salt

Reserve a little flour for rolling out the dough. Put the rest of the flour into a basin, make a well in the middle and place the water, salt and oil in it. Knead to a form a soft dough and separate it into balls (one for each crust). Roll out the dough on a floored surface.

Kolokithopita

Courgette (Zucchini Squash) Pie

- 1 kg (2.2 lb) courgettes
- 1 onion, finely chopped
- 200 gr (7 oz) feta cheese, broken in small pieces
- 1 cup grated cheese
- 3 eggs, beaten
- 2 tablespoons rusk crumbs
- 1 cup butter or margarine
- Pepper
- Pinch of salt
- 500 gr (17.6 oz) phyllo dough
- Olive oil for the baking pan and phyllo sheets

Wash the courgettes and grate them. Place them in a pot with the onion and boil until most of the liquid has evaporated. Mix them with the rest of the ingredients. Put half the phyllo dough in an oiled baking pan, brushing each sheet with oil before adding the next. Spread the filling over these and cover with the remaining sheets of dough, again oiling each one. Bake the courgette pie in a moderate oven for approximately 45 minutes.

Tiropita

Cheese Pie

- 500 gr (17.6 oz) feta cheese
- 100 gr (3.5 oz) kefalo-graviera cheese, grated
- 1 cup milk
- 5 tablespoons melted butter or margarine
- Dillweed or mint, finely chopped
- 4 eggs, beaten
- Pepper
- Butter to grease the sheets of dough
- 500 gr (17.6 oz) phyllo dough

Mash the feta cheese with a fork. Add the kefalograviera cheese, the milk, butter, dillweed or mint, eggs and pepper. Butter a baking pan and line it with half the phyllo dough, brushing each sheet with melted butter as it is added. Spread the cheese mixture over this and cover with the rest of the dough, buttering in the same way. Bake the cheese pie in a moderate oven for about an hour.

Zimi Sfoliatas

Puff Pastry

- 500 gr (17.6 oz) durum wheat flour
- 500 gr (17.6 oz) fresh cow's butter or margarine
- 1 teaspoon salt

Set a little flour aside for rolling out the dough. Sift the rest of the flour and put it in a small basin. Make a well in the middle, and add the salt, one tablespoon butter and a little water. Knead the dough on a flat surface, adding water a little at a time, until the dough stops sticking to the fingers. Shape the dough into a ball, cover it with a damp towel and leave it in the refrigerator for about half an hour. Form the remaining butter into a flat rectangular piece. Roll out the dough on a floured surface, place the butter in the middle and fold the dough over it from four sides. Roll out the dough again and fold it into three layers. Repeat this four more times, leaving the dough in the refrigerator 20 minutes after rolling it out and folding it each time.

Spanakopita

Spinach Pie

- 1 kg (2.2 lb) fresh spinach
- 300 gr (10.6 oz) spring onions, finely chopped
- 1 small bunch dillweed, finely chopped
- 1 large leek, finely chopped
- 2 eggs
- 1 cup olive oil
- Salt, pepper
- 500 gr (17.6 oz) phyllo dough

Pick, wash and blanch the spinach. Press out all excess liquid and chop it. Heat half the oil and sauté the onions and leek lightly. Remove the pot from the heat, add the dillweed, the beaten eggs, the spinach, the salt and pepper and stir to mix. Brush a baking pan with oil and line it with half the phyllo dough, brushing the sheets one by one. Add the filling and cover the pie with the remaining phyllo dough, oiling each sheet as before. Bake the spinach pie in a moderate oven for one hour.

Spinach and Cheese Pie

- 1 kg (2.2 lb) fresh spinach
- 250 gr (8.8 oz) feta cheese
- 1 large leek, finely chopped
- 300 gr (10.6 oz) spring onions, finely chopped
- 1 1/2 cup olive oil
- 1/2 bunch dillweed, finely chopped
- 1/2 bunch parsley, finely chopped
- 2 eggs
- Salt, pepper
- 500 gr (17.6 oz) phyllo dough

Pick, wash and blanch the spinach. Chop it, after squeezing out all excess liquid. Mash the feta cheese with a fork. Heat half the oil and sauté the onions and leek lightly. Remove the pot from the heat, add the dillweed, parsley, feta cheese, beaten eggs, spinach, salt and pepper, and stir to mix. Brush a baking pan with oil, and line it with half the sheets of phyllo dough, brushing each one with oil as it is added. Put in the filling and cover the pie with the rest of the dough, oiling it as before. Bake the spinach and cheese pie in a moderate oven for one hour.
Variation: Add 1/2 cup evaporated milk or fresh cream to the filling.

Chicken Pie

- 1 chicken weighing about 1 kg (2.2 lb)
- 1 whole onion
- 500 gr (17.6 oz) phyllo dough
- 1 bay leaf
- 2 level teaspoons butter
- 2 eggs, beaten
- Melted butter for brushing the sheets of dough
- Pinch of nutmeg
- 1 cup grated cheese
- 2 heaping tablespoons flour
- Salt, pepper
- Parsley or dillweed, finely chopped

Clean and wash the chicken. Put it in a pot of water, together with the whole onion and the bay leaf and let it boil until well cooked. When it has cooled, remove the skin and bones and cut the meat into small pieces. Make a white sauce with the butter, flour and 2 cups of the chicken broth, using the method for Bechamel sauce (see Sauces), but substituting chicken broth for the milk. When the sauce has cooled, add the beaten eggs, cheese, nutmeg, salt, pepper and the parsley or dillweed. Butter a baking pan and line it with half the phyllo dough, brushing each sheet with butter. Spread the filling on top of it and cover with the remaining buttered sheets of dough. Bake the chicken pie in a moderate oven for 40- 45 minutes.

Spinach and Cheese Pie ➡
Chicken Pie ➡

Leek Pie

- 1 kg (2.2 lb) leeks
- 2 eggs
- 300 gr (10.6 oz) hard feta cheese
- 1 cup olive oil
- Salt , pepper
- 500 gr (17.6 oz) phyllo dough

Cut off and discard the green parts of the leeks. Wash the white parts, chop them fine and boil them in a little water. Drain, press out excess water and add the beaten eggs, the feta cheese, mashed with a fork, half the olive oil, the salt and pepper, and stir well. Brush a baking pan with oil and line it with half the phyllo sheets, oiling each one as it is added. Add the filling and cover the pie with the remaining sheets, oiling them one by one. Bake the leek pie in a moderate oven for approximately one hour.

Kremidopita

Onion Pie

- 500 gr (17.6 oz) hard feta cheese
- 500 gr (17.6 oz) spring onions, finely chopped
- 1 small bunch dillweed, finely chopped
- 3 eggs
- Pepper
- 1/2 cup olive oil
- 2 thick pie crusts
- Melted butter

Mash the feta cheese with a fork. Add the eggs, pepper, onions, dillweed and olive oil and blend well.

Line a buttered baking pan with one of the crusts, spread the filling over it and cover with the other crust. Brush the top crust with butter and bake in a moderate oven for half an hour.

Variation: Substitute 250 gr (8.8 oz) fresh mizithra or anthotiro cheese for half the feta.

Hortopita

Greens Pie

- 1 1/2 kg (3.3 lb) various tender greens
- 3- 4 spring onions
- 250 gr (8.8 oz) feta cheese
- 1 1/2 cup olive oil
- Dillweed and parsley, finely chopped
- 4 beaten eggs
- 2 tablespoons rusk crumbs
- Pinch of salt and pepper
- 500 gr (17.6 oz) phyllo dough

Pick, wash and blanch the greens, squeeze out the excess liquid and chop them. Mash the feta cheese with a fork. Heat half the oil and sauté the onions and greens. Remove the pot from the heat and add the cheese, eggs, dillweed, parsley, crumbs, salt and pepper. Oil a baking pan and line it with half the phyllo dough, brushing each sheet with oil as it is added. Add the filling and cover the pie with the rest of the dough, oiling in the same way. Bake the greens pie in a moderate oven for approximately one hour.

Bakaliaropita

Salt Cod Pie

- 800 gr (1 3/4 lb) salt cod
- 1 cup olive oil
- 2 onions, finely chopped
- 150 gr (5.3 oz) rice
- 2 small ripe tomatoes
- 2 cloves garlic, finely chopped
- Parsley, finely chopped
- Pepper
- 2 pie crusts (not too thin)

Put the cod in water to soak the day before cooking, changing the water several times. It must soak for at least 18 hours. Remove the bones and skin and cut the cod into small pieces. Peel the tomatoes, remove the seeds and chop. Reserve a little oil for oiling the crusts and the pan, and heat the rest in a pot. Brown the onion and add the remaining ingredients, except the rice and pie crusts. Stir for a few minutes over medium heat, add the rice and cook for 1-2 minutes longer. Line an oiled baking pan with one of the crusts and fill it with the cod mixture. Cover with the second crust and brush the top with oil. Bake the pie in a moderate oven for one hour or so until the top crust is golden brown.

Note: The recipe does not call for salt because the cod is already salty. You may test the filling for salt before filling the pie and add some if necessary.

Pita me Mosharissio kai Hirino Kreas

Beef and Pork Pie

- 300 gr (10.6 oz) beef
- 300 gr (10.6 oz) pork
- 1 clove garlic, finely chopped
- 1 onion, finely chopped
- 100 gr (3.5 oz) rice
- 1/2 wineglass white wine
- 150 gr (5.3 oz) grated cheese (feta and kefalotiri)
- 2 beaten eggs
- Pepper
- 2 whole cloves
- Pinch of cinnamon
- 1 tablespoon tomato paste
- Parsley, finely chopped
- 3 tablespoons olive oil
- 2 puff pastry crusts
- A little melted butter

Cut the meat into tiny pieces. Heat the oil and sauté the onions, garlic and meat. Add the spices, stir for 1-2 minutes and add the wine, a little water and the tomato paste. Let the mixture simmer for half an hour. Next add the rice, parsley, eggs and cheese. Grease a baking pan with the butter and line it with one crust, cut to fit the pan with some overlap all around. Add the filling and cover the pie with the top crust. Fold the edge of the bottom crust up and over the edge of the top crust, to keep the filling in. Brush the pie with a little melted butter and prick it in several places with a fork. Bake in a moderate oven for one hour.

Haniotiki Tourta, a Meat Pie (Specialty of Hania, Crete)

- 1 kg (2.2 lb) lamb
- 1 kg (2.2 oz) soft fresh mizithra cheese
- Cinnamon
- 1 egg
- Sesame seeds
- Salt, pepper
- Butter to grease the pan
- 2 pie crusts

Boil the meat until well cooked. Remove the skin and bones and cut into tiny pieces. Add pepper, a little salt and a little cinnamon. Line a baking pan with one of the pie crusts. Place on it half the mizithra cheese, mashed with a fork, and a sprinkling of pepper and cinnamon. Cover the cheese with the meat. Add another layer of cheese, sprinkling again with pepper and cinnamon. Place the second crust on top, brush it with beaten egg and sprinkle sesame seeds over it. Bake the meat pie in a moderate oven for about one hour. **Variation**: Small pieces of butter may be added to the meat.

Pita Yanniotiki (Specialty of the town of Yannina)

Yannina Cheese Pie

- 650 gr (1 lb 7 oz) kefalo-graviera cheese, grated
- 500 gr (17.6 oz) milk
- 3 eggs
- Butter to grease the crusts
- 4 puff pastry crusts

Butter a baking pan, line it with one crust and brush it with melted butter. Add 1/3 of the cheese and cover it with the second buttered crust. Alternate cheese and crust until there are three layers, topping off with the crust. Brush the top of the pie with melted butter. Beat the eggs with the milk and pour them over the pie. Bake in a moderate oven until golden brown.

Kimadopita

Minced Beef Pie

- 500 gr (17.6 oz) minced beef
- 5 tablespoons butter or margarine
- 2 eggs
- 1 cup grated cheese
- 1 onion, finely chopped
- 1 tablespoon rusk crumbs
- Salt, pepper
- 1/2 cup Bechamel sauce
- 300 gr (10.6 oz) phyllo dough

Heat 2 tablespoons butter and sauté onion and minced beef. Add the salt, pepper and a little water, and let the meat simmer for an hour. Add the crumbs, the eggs and the cheese, stir and let the filling cool. Melt the rest of the butter. Put half the phyllo dough sheets in the bottom of a buttered baking pan, brushing each one with the meltered butter. Spread the meat mixture over them and cover with the remaining sheets of dough, brushing each one with butter. Bake the pie in a moderate oven until it is golden brown.

Haniotiki Tourta, a Meat Pie (Specialty of Hania, Crete) ➡
Yannina Cheese Pie ➡

PASTTA-RICE

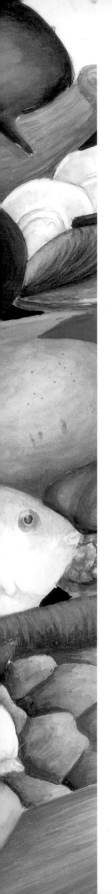

Spaghetti with Meat Sauce

SERVES 4 - 5
- 500 gr (17.6oz) spaghetti
- Salt
- 1/2 cup butter
- Grated cheese (kefalotiri, kefalograviera, or aged mizithra)
- Tomato sauce with minced meat (See Sauces)

Put on plenty of salted water to boil. When it reaches boiling point, add the spaghetti and cook, stirring from time to time. As soon as the spaghetti is done, drain it and pour the hot butter over it. Top with the meat sauce and a sprinkling of grated cheese.

Macaroni in Tomato Sauce

SERVES 4
- 500 gr (17.6oz) macaroni
- 500 gr (17.6oz) tomatoes
- 1 onion, finely chopped
- 1 clove garlic, finely chopped
- Parsley, finely chopped
- 1/2 cup olive oil
- Pinch of sugar
- 1/2 cup kefalotiri cheese, grated

Heat the oil and sauté the onion. Add the tomatoes, peeled and put through a food mill, the parsley, garlic, sugar, salt and pepper, and let the sauce simmer. Boil the macaroni in salted water, drain and add to the cooked sauce. Mix well and bring to the boil. Serve with grated cheese.

Spaghetti with Tomato Sauce

SERVES 4
- 500 gr (17.6oz) spaghetti
- Salt
- 1/2 cup butter
- Grated cheese (kefalotiri, kefalograviera, or aged mizithra)
- Tomato sauce (See Sauces)

Bring plenty of salted water to a boil and add the spaghetti. When it is tender, drain it and pour the hot butter over it. Top with the tomato sauce and sprinkle with grated cheese.

Youvetsi

Baked Manestra

SERVES 4
- 500 gr (17.6oz) manestra (rice-like pasta)
- 4 ripe tomatoes
- 3 medium onions, finely chopped
- 2 cloves garlic, finely chopped
- 1 cup olive oil
- Pinch of sugar
- 1 cup grated cheese
- Salt, pepper

Heat the oil in a pot and brown the garlic and onion. Add the tomatoes, peeled and put through a food mill, the sugar, salt and pepper, and let the sauce boil for a few minutes. Add hot water (approximately 2 1/2 cups water for each cup of manestra), and when it boils, put the sauce in an earthenware baking dish, add the manestra and bake in a pre-heated moderate oven. A short time before the manestra is completely cooked, stir it, sprinkle grated cheese over the top and continue baking until done. Serve hot.
Note: Meat broth may be used instead of water.

Makaronaki Kofto sto Fourno

Baked Macaroni

SERVES 4 - 5
- 500 gr (17.6oz) macaroni
- 150 gr (5.3 oz) melted butter
- 1/2 cup kefalotiri cheese, grated
- 200 gr (7 oz) kasseri cheese
- Salt, pepper

Boil the macaroni in salted water and drain. Add half the kefalotiri, the pepper and the butter, and stir. Put 1/3 of the macaroni into a buttered baking pan. Add half the kasseri, cut into cubes. Continue with another layer of macaroni, kasseri, and a final layer of macaroni. Sprinkle the remaining kefalotiri over the top and dot with small pieces of butter. Bake for about 15 minutes.

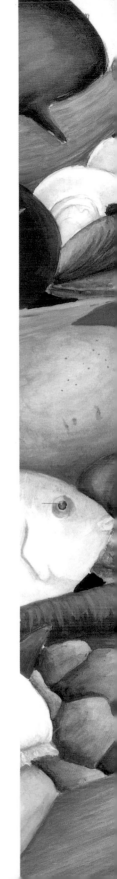

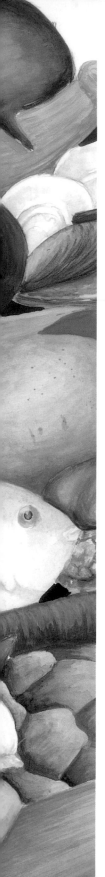

Meat and Spaghetti, a Specialty of Corfu

SERVES 4 - 5
- 1 kg (2.2 lb) veal
- 1 cup olive oil
- 1/2 cup red wine
- 4 ripe tomatoes or 1 table-spoon tomato paste
- 3 medium onions, finely chopped
- 2- 3 cloves garlic, halved
- Pinch of cinnamon
- 2 whole cloves
- Pinch of sugar
- Salt, pepper
- 500 gr (17.6 oz) thick spaghetti
- Grated cheese

Wash the meat. With the point of a knife, make slots in several places and put a piece of garlic, dredged in salt and pepper, into each slot. Heat the oil in a pot and brown the onions with the meat. Add the wine, the tomatoes, peeled and put through a food mill (or the tomato paste mixed with a little water), and the rest of the ingredients except the spaghetti and grated cheese. Let simmer for about 2 hours. Boil the spaghetti in plenty of salted water, drain and serve, topped with sauce and grated cheese. Serve the meat separately on a platter with the rest of the sauce.

Pilafi me Sikotakia

Rice with Lamb Liver

SERVES 6
- 2 cups rice
- 300 gr (10.6 oz) lamb liver
- 3 tablespoons butter
- 1 onion, finely chopped
- 1 clove garlic, finely chopped
- 1 bay leaf
- 3 ripe tomatoes
- 1/2 cup white unresinated wine
- Salt, pepper
- 3 1/2 cups meat broth (optional)

Wash and blanch the liver and cut it in small pieces. Heat one tablespoon of butter in a frying pan and sauté the liver for a few minutes. In a pot, heat one tablespoon butter and sauté the onion. Add the wine, the tomatoes, peeled and put through a food mill, the garlic, the bay leaf and the salt and pepper.

In another pot place 3 1/2 cups broth or the same amount of salted water with the rest of the butter, and bring to a boil.

Add the rice, stir, cover the pot and cook the rice over low heat for 20 minutes.

Remove the bay leaf from the sauce and add the liver. Let the sauce boil for a few minutes longer and pour over the rice.

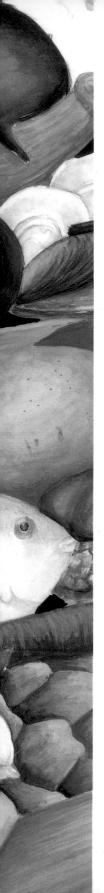

Baked Spaghetti

SERVES 6
- 500 gr (17.6oz) thick spaghetti
- 1 cup ham, finely chopped
- 2 - 3 cups Bechamel sauce (see Sauces)
- 1 cup kefalogavriera cheese, grated
- Salt

Boil the spaghetti in salted water and drain. Place it in a deep baking dish, add the ham, bechamel sauce and most of the cheese, and stir to mix. Sprinkle the rest of the cheese over the top and bake for 20 - 30 minutes.

Spaghetti with Garlic Sauce

SERVES 4
- 500 gr (17.6oz) spaghetti
- 2 cloves garlic, crushed
- 1 kg (2.2 lb) ripe tomatoes
- 1/2 cup olive oil
- Salt, pepper

Put on plenty of salted water to boil. Add the spaghetti and stir from time to time until it is done. Drain. Heat the oil and sauté the garlic. Add the tomatoes, peeled and put through a food mill, along with the salt and pepper, and let the sauce boil until thick. To serve, pour the sauce over the spaghetti.

Noodles

SERVES 4
- 500 gr (17.6oz) noodles
- 2 tablespoons butter
- 1/2 cup grated cheese
- Salt
- Tomato sauce (see Sauces)

Put water in a pot with the butter and salt. When it comes to a boil, add the noodles, cover the pot and let them simmer until they have absorbed all the water. Serve with tomato sauce and grated cheese.
Note: Use one cup of water for each cup of homemade noodles, and 1 1/2 cups water for each cup of store-bought noodles.

Pastitsio me Makaronia

Pasticcio with Macaroni

SERVES 6 - 8
- 500 gr (17.6oz) macaroni for pasticcio
- 1/2 cup butter
- Salt, pepper
- 2 eggs, beaten
- 1 1/2 cup grated cheese
- Bechamel sauce (see Sauces)
- Tomato sauce with meat (see Sauces)

Bring plenty of salted water to a boil. As soon as it reaches boiling point, put in the macaroni and stir from time to time. When the macaroni is done, drain it. Put half in a baking dish, sprinkle half the grated cheese on it and cover with the meat sauce. Then add the rest of the macaroni, sprinkle with cheese again and pour the melted butter over it. Top the pasticcio with a layer of Bechamel sauce, to which the eggs have been added. Sprinkle the rest of the cheese over the top and bake in a moderate oven for about 40 minutes.

Lahanorizo

Cabbage and Rice

SERVES 5
- 1 medium head of cabbage, finely chopped
- 1 cup rice
- 1 onion, finely chopped
- 1 cup olive oil
- Parsley, finely chopped
- Salt, pepper
- Juice of 1 lemon
- 3 ripe tomatoes

Heat the oil and sauté the cabbage and onion. Peel the tomatoes, put them through a food mill and add them, along with the salt and pepper. When the cabbage is almost done, add the rice, parsley and salt and continue to cook until the rice is tender. Serve the cabbage and rice with lemon juice.

Domatorizo

Tomatoes and Rice

SERVES 4
- 2 cups rice
- 3- 4 ripe tomatoes
- 1/2 cup olive oil
- 1 clove garlic, finely chopped
- 1 medium onion, finely chopped
- Salt, pepper

Heat the oil in a pot and sauté the garlic and onion. Add the tomatoes, peeled and put through a food mill, and let the sauce boil for a few minutes. Then add the rice, salt and pepper and stir. Cover the pot and simmer for 15- 20 minutes over very low heat.

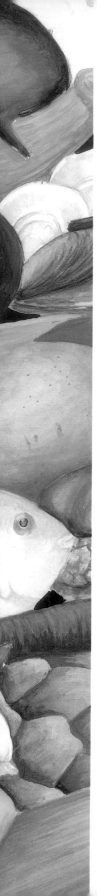

Mussels and Rice

SERVES 6
- 1 kg (2.2 lb) mussels
- 2 cups rice
- 1 medium onion, finely chopped
- 1 clove garlic, finely chopped
- 1 cup olive oil
- 3- 4 ripe tomatoes
- 1/2 cup white unresinated wine
- Salt, pepper

Scrape the mussels well, cut off their "beards" and wash them. Put them in a pot with a little water and steam them until they open. Drain and reserve the liquid. Heat the oil and sauté the garlic and onion. Add the wine first, then the tomatoes, peeled and put through a food mill, and finally the salt and pepper. Let the sauce cook for 15 minutes. Then add the liquid from the mussels, adding water if necessary, to make 4 cups in all. As soon as it comes to a boil, put in the mussels and rice and stir well. Simmer until the rice is tender.

Rice with Seafood

SERVES 6
- 2 cups rice
- 300 gr (10.6 oz) mussels
- 300 gr (10.6 oz) oysters
- 300 gr (10.6 oz) shrimp
- 1 clove garlic, finely chopped
- Salt, pepper
- Parsley, finely chopped
- 3 tablespoons olive oil

Scrape the mussels and oysters and wash them thoroughly. Cut the "beards" off the mussels. Put them in a pot with a little water and steam them until the shells open. Boil the shrimp in slightly salted water. Drain off and reserve the liquid. Heat the oil in a pot and sauté the rice and garlic lightly. Add the seafood, parsley, salt and pepper. Put in the liquid from the shrimp, with water added if necessary, to make up to 4 cups. Cover the pot and simmer for 20 minutes.

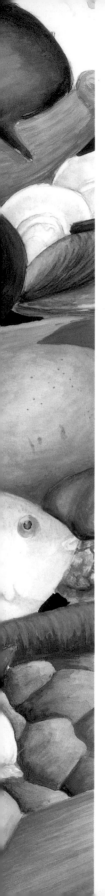

Lentils and Rice

SERVES 4
- 250 gr (8.8 oz) lentils
- 1 cup rice
- 1 cup olive oil
- 2 - 3 ripe tomatoes
- 1 onion, finely chopped
- Salt, pepper
- Pinch of cumin (optional)

Pick and wash the lentils and put them on to boil in a pot of water. When the water boils, drain them and put them into fresh water, adding the tomatoes, peeled and put through a food mill, and the salt and pepper. When the lentils are half done, add the cumin, rice and a little more hot water if needed, and simmer. Heat the oil in a frying pan and brown the onion. Pour the oil and onion over the lentils and rice and serve hot.

Spanakorizo

Spinach Rice

SERVES 6
- 1 kg (2.2 lb) spinach
- 1/2 cup rice
- 4- 5 spring onions, finely chopped
- 1 bunch parsley, finely chopped
- 3/4 cup olive oil
- Juice of 1- 2 lemons
- Salt, pepper

Pick, wash and blanch the spinach. When it has cooled, squeeze it to remove all excess liquid, and chop it up. Heat the oil in a pot and brown the onions. Add the spinach, a little water and the salt and pepper. A short time before the spinach is cooked add a little more hot water (1-1 1/2 cups) and when it comes to a boil, put in the rice and dillweed. Cover the pot and simmer for 15-20 minutes. Serve the spinach rice with lemon juice.
Variation: When adding the spinach, also add a teaspoon of tomato paste mixed in a little water.

Prassorizo

Rice with Leeks

SERVES 4
- 1 kg (2.2 lb) leeks
- 1/2 cup rice
- 1 tablespoon tomato paste
- 3/4 cup olive oil
- Dillweed, finely chopped
- Salt, pepper

Slit the leeks down the sides and wash them well. Cut them into slices. Heat the oil in a pot and brown the leeks. Add the tomato paste, mixed with a little water, the salt and pepper, and enough water to cook the leeks. Just before they are done, add some more hot water (one cup) and when it comes to a boil, add the rice and dillweed. Cover the pot and simmer for 15-20 minutes.

Lentils and Rice ➡
Spinach Rice ➡
Rice with Leeks ➡

VEGETABLES

Briam Fournou

Baked Summer Vegetables

SERVES 6 - 8
- 1 kg (2.2 lb) courgettes (zucchini squash)
- 1 kg (2.2 lb) potatoes
- 1 kg (2.2 lb) aubergines (eggplant)
- 3 onions, sliced
- 2 green peppers, cut in thin slices
- 1 kg (2.2 lb) ripe peeled tomatoes or 1 tin peeled tomatoes
- Salt, pepper
- 1 bunch parsley, finely chopped
- 1 cup olive oil

Clean and wash the courgettes, aubergines and potatoes. Cut them into slices. Put all the ingredients in a large baking pan and stir to mix. Bake the vegetables in a moderate oven for approximately 1 1/2 hours. If necessary, add a little water during cooking.
Variation: You may also add feta cheese broken into little pieces.

Melitzanes Imam Baildi

Aubergines (Eggplant) in Tomato Sauce

SERVES 5- 6
- 1 1/2 kg (3.3 lb) aubergines (long, narrow type)
- Olive oil for frying
- 6 ripe tomatoes
- 6 cloves garlic, finely chopped
- 1/2 cup olive oil
- 500 gr (17.6 oz) onions, thinly sliced
- Salt, pepper
- Parsley, finely chopped
- Pinch of sugar

Clean and wash the aubergines and make cross-shaped incisions on them. Lightly fry the whole aubergines. Heat the oil in a pot and sauté the onions. Add the tomatoes, peeled and put through a food mill, the garlic, parsley, sugar, salt and pepper, and cook for 10 minutes. Stuff the aubergines with the onion mixture. Place them in an ovenproof glass dish and pour the remaining sauce over them, adding a little water. Bake them in a moderate oven for approximately one hour. This is a dish usually served cold.

Gemista Ladera

Tomatoes and Peppers Stuffed with Rice

SERVES 6
- 7 medium tomatoes
- 6 medium green peppers
- 1 1/2 cup rice
- 2 medium onions, finely chopped
- Parsley, finely chopped
- 1 1/2 cup olive oil
- Salt, pepper
- Rusk crumbs
- 2 cups tomato juice

Wash the tomatoes and peppers. Cut a thin slice off the stem-ends and hollow out the interiors. Keep the tomato pulp, and chop it up or purée it in the blender. Mix the rice, onion, parsley, tomato pulp, 1/2 cup olive oil, salt and pepper. Fill the tomatoes and peppers with the mixture, cover them with the lids you have sliced off and arrange them in a baking pan. Pour the tomato juice and the rest of the oil over them and sprinkle the lids with rusk crumbs. Bake them in a moderate oven for 1-1 1/2 hours.

Gemista me Kima

Tomatoes and Green Peppers with Minced Meat Stuffing

SERVES 6
- 6 medium tomatoes
- 6 medium green peppers
- 1 1/2 cup olive oil
- 1 medium onion, finely chopped
- 500 gr (17.6 oz) minced beef
- 1/2 cup rice
- Parsley, finely chopped
- Salt, pepper
- Rusk crumbs
- 2 cups tomato juice

Wash the tomatoes and peppers. Cut a thin slice off the stem-ends and hollow out the interiors. Keep the tomato pulp, and chop it up or purée it in the blender. Heat 1/2 cup olive oil and sauté the onion and minced meat. Add the tomato pulp, rice, parsley, salt and pepper and simmer. Stuff the tomatoes and peppers, put their lids back on and arrange them in a baking pan. Pour the rest of the oil and the tomato juice over them and sprinkle them with the rusk crumbs. Bake in a moderate oven for approximately 1 hour.

Baked Stuffed Aubergines (Eggplant)

SERVES 8
- 1 1/2 kg (3.3 lb) medium-sized aubergines (large purple type)
- 2 onions, finely chopped
- 1 cup olive oil
- 500 gr (17.6 oz) minced beef
- Salt, pepper
- 1/2 cup white unresinated wine
- Parsley, finely chopped
- Grated cheese
- Bechamel sauce (see Sauces)

Remove the stems from the aubergines, wash and cut them in half lengthwise. Incise the cut surface, rub with salt and let stand 1/2 hour. Rinse them off, pat them dry and put them, cut side down, in a baking pan with 1 cup hot water. Bake in a moderate oven for 15 minutes or until the aubergines are soft. Sauté the onions in a pot and add the minced meat, wine and parsley. Cook the mixture for 30 minutes over low heat. Remove the seeds and part of the flesh from the aubergines, fill them with the meat mixture and top with a spoonful of Bechamel sauce. Sprinkle with grated cheese. Bake for 30 - 40 minutes.

Note: Tomato juice may be poured into the pan with the aubergines to form a sauce.

Moussakas

SERVES 6 - 8
- 3 large aubergines (large purple type)
- 1 kg (2.2 lb) potatoes
- 1 onion, finely chopped
- 1 kg (2.2 lb) minced beef
- 1/2 cup white unresinated wine
- 1/2 cup olive oil
- 2 medium ripe tomatoes
- Parsley, finely chopped
- Salt, pepper
- Olive oil for frying
- Becahmel sauce (see Sauces)

Wrap the aubergines (eggplant) in aluminium foil and bake in a moderate oven until soft. Wash and peel the potatoes, slice them and fry them lightly. Heat the oil and sauté the onion with the minced beef. Add the wine and the tomatoes, which have been peeled and put through a food mill, the parsley, salt and pepper and let the meat sauce simmer for 15 minutes. Arrange the potatoes on the bottom of a baking pan, salt them and pour the meat sauce over them. Cover with the aubergines, sliced and salted. Top with a layer of Bechamel sauce. Bake the moussakas in a moderate oven for 30 - 40 minutes.

Note: According to the traditional recipe, the aubergines are fried instead of baked. This makes for a heavier dish.

Baked Stuffed Aubergines (Eggplant) ➡
Moussakas ➡

Oven Roasted Giant Beans

SERVES 6
- 500 gr (17.6 oz) dried giant white beans
- 3/4 cup olive oil
- 4 ripe tomatoes
- Parsley, finely chopped
- Salt, pepper

The evening before cooking, put the beans in water to soak. Next day, boil them until they are tender and drain them well. Peel and chop up the tomatoes, adding the salt, pepper, oil and parsley. Spread the beans out in a baking pan and pour the sauce over them. Bake for about 40 minutes. Serve hot or cold.

Note: The sauce may be boiled for a short time before adding it to the beans.

Mushrooms in Tomato Sauce

SERVES 4
- 500 gr (17.6 oz) mushrooms chopped in large pieces
- 2- 3 medium onions
- 250 gr (8.8 oz) white unresinated wine
- 1/2 cup olive oil
- A little rosemary and dill-weed
- 1 bay leaf
- 2 cloves of garlic, finely chopped
- 1 tablespoon tomato paste
- Salt, pepper

Dissolve the tomato paste in a little water. Put it into a pot with the wine and olive oil and simmer for 10 minutes. Add the remaining ingredients and stir. Cook for about 20 minutes. Serve hot, after removing the bay leaf.

Potato Patties

SERVES 6
- 1 kg (2.2 lb) potatoes
- 300 gr (10.6 oz) grated kefalotiri cheese
- 2 eggs
- A little parsley, finely chopped
- Salt, pepper
- Olive oil for frying
- Flour

Wash and peel the potatoes. Boil them until they are soft and put them through a food mill. Place them in a bowl and add the cheese, eggs, parsley, pepper and a little salt. Knead the mixture well and shape it into patties. Dredge the patties in flour and fry them in hot oil until they are brown on both sides.

Variation: You can substitute feta cheese for the kefalotiri.

Oven Roasted Giant Beans ➡
Mushrooms in Tomato Sauce ➡

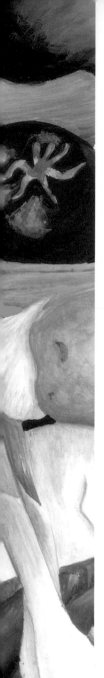

Artichokes in Olive Oil

SERVES 4
- 8 artichokes
- 8 spring onions, finely chopped
- Juice of 2 lemons
- 500 gr (17.6 oz) small potatoes
- 4 carrots, sliced
- 1/2 cup olive oil
- 1 tablespoon flour
- 1 bunch dillweed, finely chopped
- Salt, pepper

Tear the tough leaves off the artichokes and remove the fuzz from their interiors. Put them in a bowl of water, to which the juice of one lemon has been added, to keep them from turning black. Sauté the spring onions and the carrots, add the artichokes, dillweed, salt, pepper, the flour mixed with the rest of the lemon juice, and a good amount of water. When the artichokes are partially cooked, add the potatoes and continue cooking until all the vegetables are done.

Stuffed Cabbage Leaves with Egg and Lemon Sauce

SERVES 6
- 1 large head of cabbage
- 500 gr (17.6 oz) minced beef
- 1/2 cup rice
- 1 onion, finely chopped
- 1 tablespoon butter
- A little fresh dillweed
- Salt, pepper
- Egg and lemon sauce (see Sauces)

Remove the stem from the cabbage. Put it in a large pot of water and boil for 10 minutes. In a large bowl, mix the minced meat, rice, onion, dillweed, butter, salt and pepper and knead them well together. Separate the leaves of the cabbage and cut off any tough parts. Put a spoonful of the filling on each leaf, fold the sides over and roll up tightly. Line the bottom of the pot with a few cabbage leaves and arrange the cabbage rolls on top of them in circles. Place a rather heavy plate on top to keep them from opening as they boil. Cover the cabbage rolls with water and cook them over moderate heat for about one hour. Prepare the egg and lemon sauce, using the liquid from the pot. Serve hot with the egg and lemon sauce.

Cauliflower in Tomato Sauce ➡
Artichokes in Olive Oil ➡
Stuffed Cabbage Leaves with Egg and Lemon Sauce ➡

Cauliflower in Tomato Sauce

SERVES 4
- 1 1/2 kg (3.3 lb) Cauliflower
- 3 onions, finely chopped
- 1 tin peeled tomatoes
- 2 cups olive oil
- Fresh dillweed, finely chopped
- Salt, pepper

Remove the leaves and main stem from the cauliflower and separate it into flowerets. Sauté the onions in the oil, and add the tomatoes, salt, pepper and dillweed and bring to a boil. Add the cauliflower and cook for about 30 minutes. If necessary, add a little water during cooking. Serve hot or cold.

Kounoupidi me Tiri sto Fourno

Baked Cauliflower with Cheese

SERVES 4
- 1 head cauliflower, approximately 2 kg (4.4 lb)
- 4 tablespoons vinegar
- 2 cups grated graviera (gruyere) cheese
- Salt, pepper

Remove the leaves and main stem from the cauliflower and cut it in half. Wash the cauliflower thoroughly, place it in a pot with water, salt and the vinegar and boil for about 30 minutes. When it is tender remove it from the water and cut it into large pieces. Put it in a buttered glass baking dish, season with salt and pepper and pour the melted butter over it. Sprinkle the grated cheese over the top. Bake in a moderate oven until the cheese is golden brown. Serve hot. Variation: You may use a variety of cheeses instead of just graviera.

Anginares me Koukia

Artichokes with Broad Beans

SERVES 6
- 1 1/2 kg (3.3 lb) broad beans
- 6 artichokes
- 1/2 cup olive oil
- 6 spring onions, finely chopped
- 1 tin peeled tomatoes
- Fresh dillweed, finely chopped
- Salt, pepper

Wash and clean the broad beans. Remove the leaves and fuzz from the artichokes, cut them in half and rub them with lemon juice to keep them from turning black. Heat the oil in a pot and sauté the onions. Put the tomatoes through a food mill and place all the ingredients in the pot. Cover and cook for approximately one hour.

Dolmadakia Avgolemono

Stuffed Vine Leaves with Egg and Lemon Sauce

SERVES 4 - 6
- 500gr. minced beef
- 250 gr. grapevine leaves
- 1/2 cup rice
- 1 onion, finely chopped
- 1/2 cup butter
- Salt, pepper
- Eff and lemon sause (See Sauses)

Remove the steams from the vine leanes. Blanch them in salted water for 5 minutes. Let them drain for a few minutes. Put the meat, rice and onion in a bowl and knead them together to form a homogeneous mass. Put a spoonful of the filling on each leaf, fold over the sides and roll up. Arrange the stuffed vine leaves in concentric circles in a pot, add the butter and enough water to cover. Place a heavy plate on top to hold them dowm and prevent them from opening, and cook them for half an hour over medium heat. Prepare the egg the lemon sauce, using the liquid the vine leaf rolls were boiled in. Serve hot with egg and lemon sauce.
Note: If preserved vine leaves fro, a jar are used, they do not need to be blanched. They must, however, be washed well.

Oven-Roasted Potatoes with Olive Oil and Oregano

SERVES 6
- 1 1/2 kg (3.3 lb) potatoes
- 1 cup olive oil
- Juice of 1 lemon
- Oregano
- Salt, pepper

Peel and wash the potatoes and cut them into thick slices. Put them in a baking pan with the oregano, salt and pepper and mix well. Pour in the oil, lemon and 3 cups of water. Cook the potatoes in a moderate oven for approximately one hour.

Peppers in Sauce

SERVES 5
- 1 kg (2.2 lb) sweet yellow peppers (long, tapering type)
- 4 ripe tomatoes, peeled and put through a food mill
- Salt, pepper, vinegar
- Olive oil for frying

Wash the peppers, pat them dry and prick them with a fork. Heat the oil and fry them until they are brown. Put the tomatoes, oil, salt and pepper in a pot and cook until all the liquid has evaporated. Arrange the peppers on a platter or ovenproof dish and sprinkle them with salt and a liberal amount of vinegar. Pour the sauce over them and serve hot or cold.

Mashed Potatoes

SERVES 4
- 1 kg (2.2 lb) potatoes
- Salt
- 1 cup hot milk
- 3 tablespoons fresh butter

Wash and peel the potatoes. Boil them in salty water until they are soft. Put them through a food mill. Put the butter in a pot with the potatoes and stir to mix. Add the milk a little at a time to continue stirring with a wooden spoon. Add little by little the liquid in which the potatoes were boiled until the mashed potatoes are the consistency of soft pudding.

Oven-Roasted Potatoes with Olive Oil and Oregano ➡
Peppers in Sauce ➡

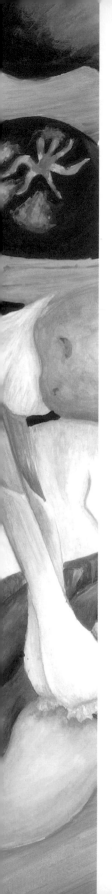

Potatoes in Tomato Sauce

SERVES 6
- 1 1/2 kg (3.3 lb) small round potatoes
- 1 large onion, finely chopped
- 4 ripe tomatoes or 1 tin peeled tomatoes
- 1/2 cup olive oil
- 1 clove garlic, cut quarters
- Salt, pepper

Peel, wash and cut any larger potatoes into pieces the size of smaller ones. In a pot, heat the oil and brown the onion. Add the tomatoes, peeled and put through a food mill, the garlic, salt, pepper and three cups water and let cook until the potatoes are tender and the sauce has thickened.

Yellow Split Pea Purée, a Specialty of Santorini

SERVES 8
- 500 gr (17.6 oz) yellow split peas
- 1 medium onion
- 1/2 cup olive oil
- Salt, pepper
- Parsley, finely chopped
- Onion, finely chopped
- Juice of 1 lemon

Wash the split peas, place them in a pot, cover with water and let them boil. Skim off the scum that forms on the top of the water. Add the onion, quartered, a little salt, half the olive oil, and let simmer for about an hour until the peas are soft and have acquired the consistency of thick porridge. Put the split peas through a food mill until they are a smooth purée. Add the rest of the oil, the lemon juice, the finely chopped onion and a little more salt. Stir and garnish with finely chopped parsley.

Potatoes in Tomato Sauce ➡
Yellow Split Pea Purée,
a Specialty of Santorini ➡

Green Beans and Potatoes in Olive Oil

SERVES 6
- 1 kg (2.2 lb) fresh green beans
- 1 large onion, grated
- 4 potatoes
- 4 ripe tomatoes or 1 tin peeled chopped tomatoes
- A little grated garlic
- Parsley, finely chopped
- Salt, pepper
- Pinch of sugar

Clean and wash the beans thoroughly. Heat the oil in a pot and sauté the onion. Add the remaining ingredients except the potatoes, along with a little water, and let simmer for 20 minutes, then add the potatoes, cut into quarters. If necessary, add a little more water and cook until well done. Serve lukewarm.

Variation: The sauteing of the onion may be omitted and all the ingredients placed in the pot at once. This makes the dish lighter.

Peas with Butter

SERVES 6
- 1 1/2 kg (3.3 lb) fresh peas
- 4 - 5 spring onions, finely chopped
- 1/2 cup butter
- 3 ripe tomatoes
- 1 bunch dillweed, finely chopped
- Salt, pepper
- Pinch of sugar

Shell and wash the peas. Put them in a pot with a little water and a pinch of sugar, and boil them for 15 minutes. Sauté the onions in the butter and add the dillweed, pepper and tomatoes, which have been peeled and put through a food mill. When the sauce comes to a boil, add the peas and let them cook over low heat for 1/2 hour.

Variation: You can add 3 - 4 carrots or 1/2 kg (1.1 lb) potatoes cut in large pieces.

Okra in Olive Oil

SERVES 6
- 1 kg (2.2 lb) okra
- 1 cup olive oil
- 2 onions, finely chopped
- 4 ripe tomatoes
- Salt, pepper
- Vinegar

Trim the tops from okra, wash well, sprinkle with vinegar and let stand for one hour. Rinse well and drain. Put the oil in a pot and sauté the onions and okra. Add the tomatoes, peeled and put through a food mill, the salt, pepper and a little water. Cook over medium heat until all the water has evaporated.

Note: Okra must not be stirred as it will break up.

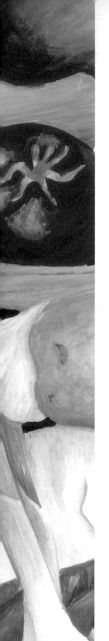

Giant Beans in Tomato Sauce

SERVES 6
- 500 gr (17.6 oz) dried white beans (giant size)
- 1 cup olive oil
- 3 onions, finely chopped
- 3 carrots, sliced
- 1/2 tin peeled and chopped tomatoes
- Salt, pepper
- Parsley, finely chopped

The evening before cooking, put the beans in water to soak. Next morning, boil them in plenty of water for about an hour, or until tender. Place the tomatoes, onions, carrots, parsley, oil, salt and pepper, in a pot and simmer the sauce for half an hour. Put the beans in the pot with the sauce and cook for a few minutes.

Cabbage with Butter

SERVES 4
- 1 medium head of cabbage
- 1/2 cup butter
- 3 tablespoons vinegar
- 1 onion, finely chopped
- Whole peppercorns
- Salt, pepper, paprika
- 1/2 cup white wine

Remove the tough parts of the cabbage, cut it in quarters and then into strips. Wash and drain the cabbage and put it in a pot with the rest of the ingredients and a cup of water. Simmer over low heat until the water has evaporated.

Tomato Patties, a Specialty of Santorini

SERVES 4
- 500 gr (17.6 oz) ripe tomatoes
- 2 onions, finely chopped
- Mint and parsley, finely chopped
- Salt, pepper
- Flour
- Olive oil for frying

Peel and chop the tomatoes. Put them in a bowl along with the onions, mint, parsley salt and pepper, and mix well. Add flour until the mixture is soft but firm. Shape into patties. Put the oil in a frying pan, let it get very hot and put in the patties. Turn down the heat a little and let them brown on both sides, Serve hot.
Variation: You may add grated cheese to the mixture

Melitzanes Laderes

Aubergines (Eggplant) in Olive Oil

SERVES 5
- 1 1/2 kg (3.3 lb) aubergines (long, narrow type)
- 4 ripe tomatoes, peeled and chopped fine
- 4 onions, finely chopped
- 1 bunch parsley, finely chopped
- 150 gr (5.3 oz) olive oil
- 1 whole bulb of garlic, finely chopped
- Salt, pepper
- Pinch of sugar

Clean the aubergines, cut them into pieces, rub them all over with plenty of salt and let them stand for about an hour. Put half the olive oil in a pot and sauté the onions. Add the tomatoes, parsley, garlic and pepper, and simmer. Rinse the aubergines in plenty of water and let them drain. Put the rest of the oil in a frying pan and when it is hot, fry the aubergines lightly.

Put the aubergines into the sauce and add water until they are half covered. Let them cook over low heat until the sauce is thick.

Melitzanes Tiganites me Saltsa Domatas

Fried Aubergines (Eggplant) with Tomato Sauce

SERVES 5
- 1 1/2 kg (3.3 lb) aubergines (large purple type)
- 1/2 cup olive oil
- 6 ripe tomatoes
- 6 cloves garlic, finely chopped
- 1 teaspoon sugar
- A little flour
- A little white unresinated wine
- Salt, pepper
- Olive oil for frying

Cut the aubergines into round slices, rub them with plenty of salt and let them stand for approximately 1/2 hour. Rinse them off and set them aside to drain well. Dredge the aubergine slices in flour and fry until golden brown. Heat the 1/2 cup olive oil in a frying pan, sauté the garlic lightly and add the wine.

Add the tomatoes, peeled and put through a food mill, the sugar, salt and pepper and cook over medium heat until the sauce has thickened. Place the aubergines in a small metal or ovenproof glass dish and bake in a moderate heat for about 20 minutes, or until the aubergines have absorbed the sauce.

FISH-SEAFOOD

Stuffed Squid

SERVES 6
- 1 kg (2.2 lb) medium-sized squid
- 1 cup rice
- 3 medium onions, finely chopped
- Mint, finely chopped
- Parsley, finely chopped
- Pinch of sugar
- 2- 3 tomatoes
- 1 cup olive oil
- Salt, pepper
- 2/3 cup white unresinated wine

Clean and wash the squid, and separate the tentacles from the bodies. Set the bodies aside and chop the tentacles fine. Heat a little olive oil and brown the onions. Add the parsley, mint, the squid tentacles, the tomatoes, peeled and put through a food mill, and the sugar and let the sauce simmer. Put in the rice, let boil for a few minutes and remove from the head. Stuff the squid bodies with the mixture and sew them shut. Place them in a baking pan, pour the rest of the oil, the wine and a little water over them, and bake in a moderate oven for 25 minutes.

Stuffed Mussels, a Specialty of Constantinople

SERVES 6
- 1 kg (2.2 lb) large mussels
- 1 cup olive oil
- 2 medium onions, finely chopped
- 1 cup rice
- 2 tablespoons pine nuts
- 2 tablespoons raisins
- Salt, pepper

Discard any mussels whose shells are open or broken. Rub those with closed shells with a stiff brush and cut their "beards". Wash them well under running water and drain them. Put them in a pot with a little water and steam until the shells open. Heat half the oil in a frying pan, steam until the shells open. Heat half the oil in a frying pan and sauté the onions lightly. Add the rice and sauté together for 1 - 2 minutes. Pour in a cup of the liquid in which the mussels were steamed (adding water if it is less than one cup), and add the salt, pepper, raisins and pine nuts. Boil the mixture for 5 minutes. Fill the mussels with the stuffing and put them into a pot with the rest oil and 1 1/2 cup hot water. Cook over low heat until the rice is tender.

Variation: Add finely chopped parsley and mint to the filling.

Barbounia Marinata

Marinated Red Mullet

SERVES 5
- 1 kg (2.2 lb) red mullet
- Lemon juice
- Flour for frying
- Olive oil for frying
- Salt, pepper
- Marinade sauce for fish
- (see Sauces)

Mix the salt and pepper with the flour. Clean and wash the fish, sprinkle the lemon juice over them and leave them for 15 minutes. Dredge the fish in the flour and fry them in hot oil. Prepare the marinade sauce with 1/2 cup of the oil in which the fish were fried and pour it over the fish.

Barbounia me Saltsa Domatas

Red Mullet in Tomato Sauce

SERVES 5
- 1 kg (2.2 lb) red mullet
- Flour for frying
- Salt, pepper
- Juice of 1 lemon
- Olive oil for frying
- 1/2 cup olive oil
- 4 ripe tomatoes
- 1 clove garlic
- 1/2 cup white wine

Mix the flour, salt and pepper. Clean and wash the fish, sprinkle them with the lemon juice, dredge them in the flour and fry. Heat the oil and add the tomatoes, peeled and put through a food mill, the garlic and the wine, and simmer the sauce for 30 minutes. Place the fish in a baking pan, pour the sauce over them and bake in a moderate oven for 15 minutes

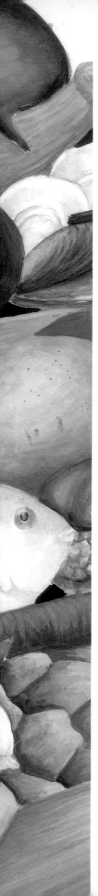

Baked Fish

SERVES 4
- 1 kg (2.2 lb) fish (dentex, grouper, tunny, etc.), sliced into steaks
- 1/2 cup olive oil
- Salt, pepper
- Oregano

Wash the fish steaks, season with salt and pepper, rub them with oil and sprinkle oregano over them. Place them in an oiled baking pan and bake in a moderate oven for 35 - 40 minutes.

Marinated Fish

SERVES 5
- 1 kg (2.2 lb) middle-sized fish (bogues, pandoras, red mullet)
- Flour
- Salt, pepper
- Olive oil for frying
- Marinade sauce for fish (see Sauces)

Mix the flour with the salt and pepper. Clean and wash the fish, dredge them in flour and fry in hot oil. Strain the oil from the frying pan. Use 1/2 cup of this oil in preparing the marinade sauce. Serve the fish hot or cold.

Baked Fish ➡
Marinated Fish ➡

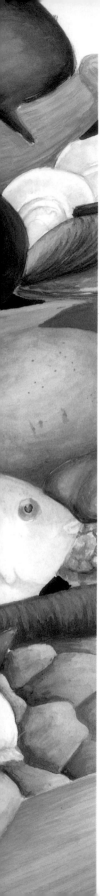

Grilled Lobster

SERVES 4
- 2 lobsters, cut in half lengthwise
- Juice of 1 lemon
- Salt, pepper

Season the lobster halves with salt and pepper and place them on a hot grill, shell side down. Grill the lobsters for about 20 minutes, turn them over and grill for another 20 minutes. Serve with lemon juice or olive oil and lemon juice.

Astakos Vrastos

Boiled Lobster

SERVES 4 - 6
- 1 large lobster
- 1 stalk of celery
- 1 carrot, sliced
- 1 onion, sliced
- 1 bay leaf
- 1 demitasse cup vinegar
- Salt
- Olive oil and lemon juice

Bring plenty of water to boil in a large pot to which the vegetables, bay leaf, vinegar and salt have been added. As soon as it comes to a boil, put in the lobster, cover the pot and cook until done. Remove the meat from the lobster, cut it in slices and pour the oil and lemon over it.

Note: 1. If the lobster is still alive, tie its tail to its body.

2. A 1-kg (2.2 lb) lobster requires about 30 minutes to cook. Figure on 10 minutes for each additional kg (2.2 lb).

Variation: If the lobster has coral (eggs), you may add these to the oil and lemon dressing.

Astakos me Saltsa Domatas

Lobster in Tomato Sauce

SERVES 4 - 6
- 1 large boiled lobster (see Boiled Lobster)
- 3 - 4 ripe tomatoes
- 1/2 cup olive oil
- 2 medium onions, sliced
- Parsley, finely chopped
- 1 1/2 cup of the liquidin which the lobster was boiled
- Salt, pepper

Remove the meat from the lobster and cut it in slices. Heat the oil in a pot and brown the onions. Add the tomatoes, peeled and put through a food mill, together with all the other ingredients, except the lobster, and simmer the sauce. When it has thickened, add the lobster, let it boil for a few moments and serve immediately.

Marides me Saltsa Domatas

Whitebait in Tomato Sauce

SERVES 3 - 4
- 500 gr (17.6 oz) of the smallest whitebait
- 4 - 5 ripe tomatoes
- 2 cloves garlic, finely chopped
- Parsley, finely chopped
- 2 tablespoons vinegar
- 1/2 cup olive oil
- Salt, pepper
- Olive oil for frying

Wash the fish, flour them and fry them in plenty of hot oil. Peel the tomatoes and put them through a food mill. Place them in a pot, together with the garlic, parsley, vinegar, salt and pepper, and cook the sauce over low heat. Pour the sauce over the fish and serve.

Kalamarakia Tiganita

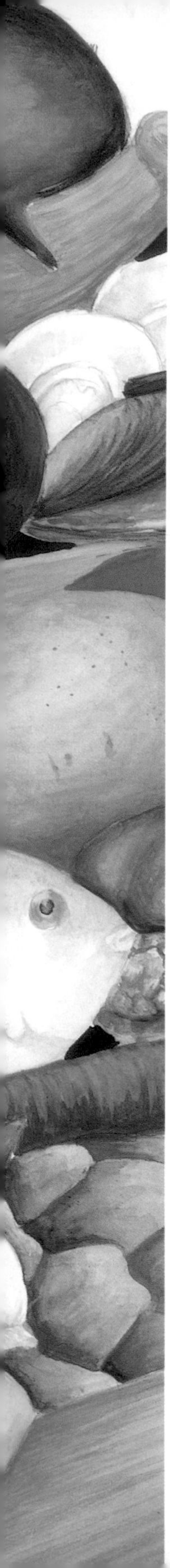

Fried Squid

SERVES 4
- 1 kg (2.2 lb) small squid
- Flour
- Salt
- Olive oil for frying
- 2 lemons, halved

Mix the flour with the salt. Clean and wash the squid, dredge them in flour and fry in hot oil, turning them carefully so they brown on all sides. Serve garnished with the lemon halves.

Galeos Tiganitos me Skordalia

Fried Tope with Garlic Sauce

SERVES 5
- 1 kg (2.2 lb) tope, sliced into steaks
- Juice of 1 lemon
- Flour for frying
- Olive oil for frying
- Salt, pepper
- Garlic sauce (see Salads)

Mix the flour with the salt and pepper. Wash the fish steaks and sprinkle them with lemon juice. Dredge them in flour and fry them in plenty of hot oil. Dress with the garlic sauce and serve

Marides Tiganites

Fried Whitebait

SERVES 4
- 500 gr (17.6 oz) whitebait
- 1 cup flour
- 2 lemons, quartered
- Olive oil for frying
- Salt

Wash the fish, dip them in flour and fry in plenty of hot oil. Season with the lemon quarters and serve hot.

Fried Squid ➡
Fried Tope with Garlic Sauce ➡
Fried Whitebait ➡

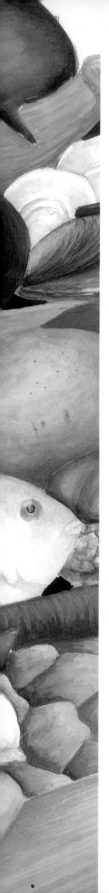

Karavides Ladolemono

Crayfish with Oil and Lemon Dressing

SERVES 6
- 1 kg (2.2 lb) crayfish
- Celery
- 1 medium onion, sliced
- Juice of half a lemon
- Salt
- Oil and lemon dressing (see Sauces)

Wash the crayfish. Place a little celery, the onion and lemon juice in a pot. Add water and salt and boil for 10 minutes. Add the crayfish and continue to cook over low heat for approximately 20 minutes. Drain the crayfish and serve with oil and lemon dressing.

Gavros sto Fourno

Baked Fresh Anchovies

SERVES 4
- 1 kg (2.2 lb) fresh anchovies
- 1 teaspoon oregano
- 1 cup olive oil
- Juice of 2 lemons
- Salt, pepper

Clean the anchovies, cut off and discard their heads and wash them thoroughly. Arrange the anchovies in a baking pan with the rest of the ingredients and a little water, and bake in a moderate oven for 40 - 45 minutes

Midia Tiganita

Fried Mussels

SERVES 4
- 1 kg (2.2 lb) mussels
- 1 cup beer
- flour
- Olive oil for frying

Clean and wash the mussels as in the above recipe, "Stuffed Mussels". Remove the mussels from their shells. Dredge them in flour, dip each one in the beer and fry in plenty of hot oil. Serve hot.

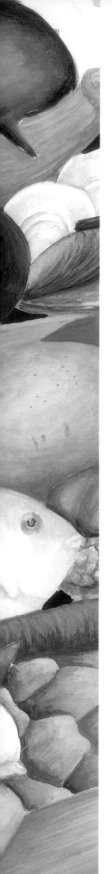

Grilled Fish

SERVES 4
- 1 kg (2.2 lb) large fish (pandoras, saddled bream, grouper, etc.)
- Oil and lemon dressing
- Finely chopped parsley or oregano

Clean and wash the fish. Rub them with oil and lemon dressing and cook them under a hot grill. Serve with oil and lemon dressing to which finely chopped parsley or oregano has been added.

Fish Baked in Tomato Sauce

SERVES 6
- 1 1/2 kg (3.3 lb) fish (dentex, grouper, sea bream, etc.), sliced into steaks
- Juice of 1 lemon
- 6 ripe tomatoes
- 1 tablespoon tomato paste
- 3 cloves garlic, finely chopped
- Parsley, finely chopped
- 1 cup olive oil
- Salt, pepper
- Rusk crumbs

Wash the fish, sprinkle it with lemon juice, salt and pepper and place it in a baking pan. Peel half the tomatoes and put them through a food mill. Add the tomato paste dissolved in a little water, the garlic, parsley, olive oil, salt and pepper and stir. Pour the mixture over the fish. Slice the remaining tomatoes, place them on top of the fish, sprinkle with the rusk crumbs and bake in a moderate oven for about 40 minutes.

Boiled Fish

SERVES 4
- 1 kg (2.2 lb) fish suitable for boiling (dentex, sea bream, fresh cod, etc.)
- Juice of 1 lemon
- 2 carrots
- 1 medium onion
- Celery
- Parsley
- Red pepper
- Salt
- Oil and lemon dressing (see Sauces)
- To garnish: Boiled mixed vegetables (potatoes, carrots, courgettes, beets)

Clean and wash the fish. Place all the ingredients except the fish in a pot of water. Boil for another 20 minutes. Add the fish and continue to simmer for 20 minutes. Garnish with the boiled vegetables and serve with oil and lemon dressing.

Grilled Fish ➡
Fish Baked in Tomato Sauce ➡

Soupies me Spanaki

Cuttlefish with Spinach

SERVES 5
- 1 kg (2.2 lb) cuttlefish
- 1 cup olive oil
- 2 medium onions, sliced
- 1 clove garlic, finely chopped
- 3 - 4 ripe tomatoes or 1 tin peeled tomatoes
- Salt, pepper
- Parsley, finely chopped
- 1 kg (2.2 lb) spinach

Clean and wash the cuttle fish and cut them into small pieces. Heat the oil and sauté the onions and garlic. Add the cuttlefish, continuing to sauté for afew minutes. Then add the tomatoes, peeled and put through a food mill, the salt and pepper, and simmer for 1 1/2 hours. Pick and wash the spinach, blanch it and chop it. Just before the cuttlefish are done, add the spinach and parsley and cook for a few minutes before serving.

Garides me Kokini Saltsa kai Pilafi

Shrimp with Tomato Sauce and Rice

SERVES 5
- 1 kg (2.2 lb) shrimp
- Juice of half a lemon
- 1/2 cup olive oil
- 2 medium onions, finely chopped
- 1 clove garlic, finely chopped
- 3 - 4 tomatoes
- Pinch of sugar
- Salt, pepper, paprika
- 2 cups rice

Clean and wash the shrimp and simmer them for 5 minutes in water to which the lemon juice has been added. Drain them, reserving the liquid. Heat the oil and sauté the onion and garlic lightly. Add the tomatoes, peeled and put through a food mill, the parsley, sugar, salt, pepper and paprika and let the sauce simmer. Five minutes before removing from the heat, add the shrimp. Make up the liquid in which the shrimp were boiled to 3 1/2 cups with water. Add salt and put it on to boil. When it comes to a boil, add the rice, stir, cover the pot, reduce heat to a minimum and let the rice simmer for 20 minutes. Pour the sauce over the rice and serve.

Cuttlefish with Spinach ➡
Shrimp with Tomato Sauce and Rice ➡

Bakaliaros Pastos Tiganitos

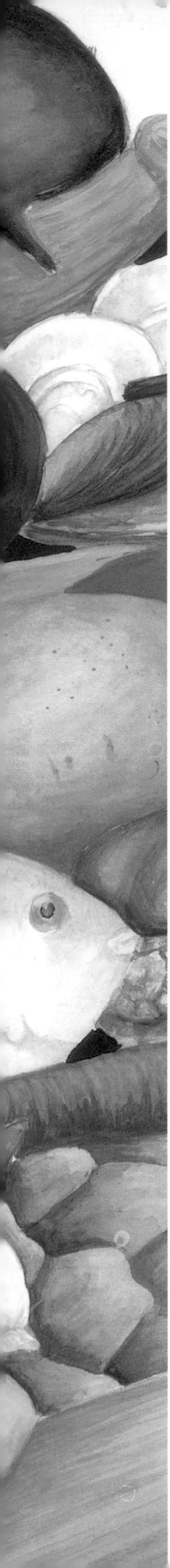

Fried Salt Cod

SERVES 4
- 500 gr (17.6 oz) salt cod
- 1 cup flour
- 1 egg, beaten
- Olive oil for frying
- Salt

The day before cooking, cut the cod into pieces and put it in plenty of water to soak. Change the water several times. Next day, remove the skin from the cod. Mix the flour with the salt, egg and water to make a thin batter. Dip each piece of fish in the batter and fry in hot oil.

Bakaliaros Pastos Plaki

Salt Cod in Tomato Sauce

SERVES 4
- 1 salt cod
- 1 kg (2.2 lb) potatoes
- 1 cup olive oil
- 2 medium onions, finely chopped
- 4 ripe tomatoes
- 3 cloves garlic, finely chopped
- 1 bunch parsley, finely chopped
- Salt, pepper

The day before cooking, cut the cod in pieces and put it in plenty of water to soak. Change the water several times. Next day, drain the cod and remove the skin. Peel the potatoes and cut them into thin slices. Heat the oil and brown the onions. Add the tomatoes, peeled and put through a food mill, the garlic, parsley, salt and pepper. Arrange the potato slices in the bottom of a baking pan. Pour half the sauce over them, add the fish, and top with the rest of the sauce. Bake in a moderate oven for about 30 minutes.

Kolii Psiti sto Fourno

Oven-Baked Spanish Mackerel

SERVES 4
- 1 kg Spanish mackerel
- 2 medium onions, finely chopped
- 3 ripe tomatoes
- 3 cloves garlic, finely chopped
- Salt, pepper
- Oregano
- 1 cup olive oil

Clean, wash and salt the fish. Peel the tomatoes, chop them up fine and mix them with the rest of the ingredients, except the oil. Stuff the body cavities of the mackerel with the mixture. Arrange the fish in a baking pan, pour the olive oil over them and bake them in a moderate oven for approximately 40 minutes.

Lithrinia me Krassi

Pandoras in Wine

SERVES 6
- 1 1/2 kg (3.3 lb) Pandoras
- 1/2 cup olive oil
- 3 small onions, sliced
- 3 - 4 ripe tomatoes
- 1 clove garlic, finely chopped
- Parsley, finely chopped
- 1 wineglass white unresinated wine
- Salt, pepper

Clean and wash the fish and place them in a baking pan. Heat the oil and sauté the onions. Add the tomatoes, peeled and put through a food mill, the garlic, parsley, salt, pepper and wine and cook the sauce for 30 minutes. Pour it over the fish and bake in a moderate oven for 30 minutes.

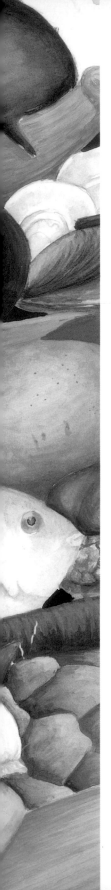

Garides Ladolemono

Shrimp with Oil and Lemon Dressing

SERVES 4
- 1 kg (2.2 lb) shrimp
- 1 stalk of celery
- Juice of half a lemon
- 1 small onion, sliced
- Salt
- Oil and lemon dressing with mustard (see Sauces)

Wash the shrimp. Put 4 cups water into a pot with the celery, onion, lemon juice and salt, and boil for 10 minutes. Add the shrimp and simmer for another 10 minutes. Drain and clean the shrimp and pour the oil and lemon dressing over them.

Oktapodi me Makaronaki Kofto

Octopus with Macaroni

SERVES 6
- 1 1/2 kg (3.3 lb) octopus
- 1 cup olive oil
- 1 medium onion, finely chopped
- 1 clove garlic, finely chopped
- 1 wineglass white unresinated wine
- 3 - 4 ripe tomatoes or 1 tin peeled tomatoes
- 500 gr (17.6 oz) macaroni

Wash the octopus, place it in a pot (no water is necessary) and let it simmer until most of its juices have evaporated. Drain the octopus and cut it into small pieces. Heat the oil and sauté the onion, garlic and octopus pieces. Add the wine, the tomatoes, peeled and put through a food mill, the salt and pepper and cook over low heat. Add some more water and when it comes to a boil, add the macaroni. Serve when the macaroni is tender.

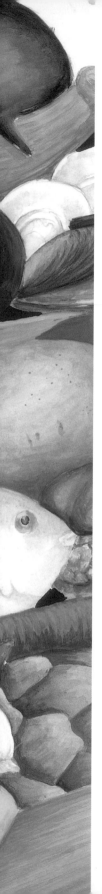

Baked Octopus, a Specialty of Thessaly

SERVES 6
- 1 1/2 kg (3.3 lb) octopus
- 8 cloves garlic
- 8 bay leaves
- Parsley, finely chopped
- Oil and vinegar

Wash the octopus. Place it on a large sheet of waxed paper and wrap up a clove of garlic and a bay leaf in each tentacle. Sprinkle the octopus with finely chopped parsley, wrap it in the waxed paper and place it in a baking pan. Pour a glass of water over it and bake it in a moderate oven for one hour. Serve with oil and vinegar dressing.

Oktapodi Vrasto

Boiled Octopus

SERVES 6 - 8
- 1 1/2 kg (3.3 lb) octopus
- 3 cloves of garlic, mashed to a paste
- Parsley, finely chopped
- Oregano
- Pepper
- 3/4 cup olive oil
- 1/2 cup vinegar

Wash the octopus and place it in a pot. Cook it over low heat until it is tender: no water need be added. Cut it into small pieces. Put the rest of the ingredients into a small glass jar, put the lid on and shake well. Pour the sauce over the octopus. It may be kept in a closed container in the refrigerator for several days.

Oktapodi Stifado

Octopus Stew with Tiny Onions

SERVES 6
- 1 1/2 kg (3.3 lb) octopus
- 1 cup olive oil
- 1 medium onion, finely chopped
- 1 clove garlic, finely chopped
- 1 wineglass white unresinated wine
- 3 - 4 ripe tomatoes or 1 tin peeled tomatoes
- 1 kg (2.2 lb) tiny onions
- 3 tablespoons vinegar
- 1 bay leaf

Wash the octopus, place it in a pot and let it simmer until tender. It is not necessary to add water. Drain the octopus and cut into small pieces. Heat the oil and sauté the onion, garlic and octopus. Add the wine, the tomatoes, peeled and put through a food mill, the onions, peeled and washed, the vinegar and the bay leaf. Let simmer until most of the liquid has evaporated.

Note: After peeling the onions, cut a small cross into the root end to keep them from splitting open as they boil.

Garides Tiganites

Fried Shrimp

SERVES 4
- 500 gr (17.6 oz) peeled shrimp
- 1 cup flour
- Salt, pepper
- Olive oil for frying
- 1 lemon, sliced

Mix the flour with the salt and pepper. Dredge the shrimp in flour and fry them in plenty of hot oil. Serve the shrimp garnished with slices of lemon.

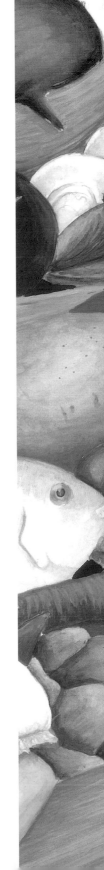

POULTRY-GAME

Stuffed Turkey

SERVES 10 - 12
- 1 turkey, approximately 5 kgs (11 lb)
- 500 gr (17.6 oz) minced beef
- 10 chestnuts, roasted and broken in pieces
- 50 gr (1.8 oz) pine nuts
- 2 medium onions, finely chopped
- 4 tablespoons white wine or brandy
- Salt, pepper
- Butter or margarine
- 1 lemon

Clean and wash the turkey, rub it with lemon inside and out and season it with salt and pepper.

Heat a little butter, sauté the minced beef with the onion, and add the wine or brandy. Add the chestnuts, pine nuts, rice, salt and pepper, stir to mix and remove the pot from the heat. Fill the turkey's body cavity with the stuffing and sew it shut. Baste with butter and roast in a moderate oven for 4 - 5 hours.

Duck with Peas

SERVES 5 - 6
- 1 duck up to 1 1/2 kg (3.3 lb)
- 1/2 cup butter or margarine
- 1 onion, finely chopped
- 4 ripe tomatoes
- 500 gr (17.6 oz) peas
- Parsley, finely chopped
- Salt, pepper
- Pinch of sugar

Singe and wash the duck. Cut it into serving pieces and season with salt and pepper.

Heat the butter in a pot and brown the duck with the onion. Add the tomatoes, peeled and put through a food mill, the sugar and a few table-spoons of water, and let the duck cook slowly for 1 1/2 - 2 hours. Shell and wash the peas. Bring a little salted water to the boil, add the peas and cook until tender. When the duck is almost done, add the peas and the parsley and continue cooking for a few more minutes.

Kotopoulo me Hilopites

Chicken and Noodles

SERVES 4
- 1 medium-sized chicken
- 2 cups noodles
- 4 ripe tomatoes
- 2 onions, finely chopped
- 1/2 cup olive oil
- Pinch of oregano
- 1 green pepper, finely chopped
- 1 clove garlic, finely chopped
- Salt, pepper

Clean and wash the chicken and cut it into serving pieces. Put the tomatoes through a food mill. Heat the oil in a pot and sauté the chicken with the onions. Add the tomatoes, salt, pepper, oregano, green pepper and garlic and cook over low heat. Remove the chicken from the pot and keep it hot. Add 1 1/2 cups water to the sauce and when it comes to a boil put in the noodles. When the noodles are almost done, put the chicken back into the pot, bring to a boil again and serve.

Kotopoulo Gemisto me Lahano Toursi

Stuffed Chicken with Sauerkraut

SERVES 5 - 6
- 1 chicken 1 1/2 kg (3.3 lb) with giblets
- 250 gr (8.8 oz) minced beef
- 1 onions, finely chopped
- 1 1/2 kg (3.3 lb) sauerkraut
- 3 tablespoons butter
- 2 tablespoons raisins
- 6 roasted chestnuts, broken into pieces
- 2 tablespoons rice
- Pepper

Drain the sauerkraut, press out the excess liquid and chop it fine. Heat a tablespoon of the butter, sauté the sauerkraut and place it in a baking pan.

Clean and wash the chicken and season with pepper. Heat another tablespoon of the butter and sauté the onion, the minced beef and the chicken giblets, finely chopped. Add a little water and let the mixture cook over low heat for 15 minutes. Add the raisins, chestnuts and rice, and stir well. Stuff the chicken's body cavity with the mixture and sew it shut. Baste the chicken with the rest of the butter and place it in the pan on top of the sauerkraut. Roast in a moderate oven for 1 1/2 hours.

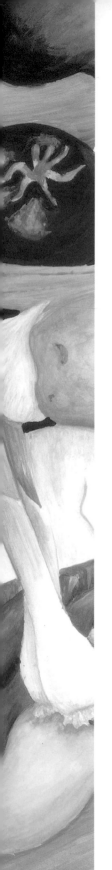

Oven-Roasted Chicken

SERVES 5 - 6
- 1 chicken about 1 1/2 kgs (3.3 lb)
- 1 kg (2.2 lb) small round potatoes
- Juice of 2 lemons
- 1 cup olive oil
- 1 tablespoon mustard
- Thyme
- Salt, pepper

Wash the chicken thoroughly and rub it inside and out with salt, pepper and lemon juice. Rub the whole chicken with mustard. Peel and wash the potatoes. Place them in a roasting pan, season with salt, pepper and thyme and pour in the lemon juice, oil and a little water. Roast the chicken and potatoes in a moderate oven for 1 1/2 hours, turning the chicken over so that it browns on both sides.

Ortikia Scharas

Grilled Quail

SERVES 4
- 1 large quail
- 1/2 cup olive oil
- 2 - 3 cloves garlic, sliced
- Salt, pepper

Pluck, singe and wash the quail. Cut through their breastbones, open them and pound them to flatten them out. Cut small slits in the quail meat and insert a slice of garlic, dredged in salt and pepper, in each slit. Season the quail with salt and pepper, brush them with oil and cook on the grill, turning from time to time.

Kotopoulo me Bamies

Chicken with Okra

SERVES 4 - 5
- 1 medium-sized chicken
- 500 gr (17.6 oz) okra
- 1 cup olive oil
- 4 - 5 ripe tomatoes or 1 tin peeled tomatoes
- 1 large onion, sliced
- Salt, pepper
- 2 - 3 tablespoons vinegar for the okra
- Parsley, finely chopped

Clean and wash the chicken and cut it into serving pieces. Heat the oil in a pot and brown the chicken pieces with the onions. Add the chopped tomatoes, salt and pepper and simmer. Trim the okra and wash it thoroughly, salt it, sprinkle the vinegar over it and let it stand for about 15 minutes. When the chicken is partially cooked, rinse the okra and add it to the chicken, together with the parsley. Cook until the sauce is thick.
Note: Do not stir the okra while cooking, as it tends to break up.

Oven-Roasted Chicken ➡
Grilled Quail ➡
Chicken with Okra ➡

Fried Chicken

SERVES 4 - 5
- 1 chicken about 1 1/2 kgs (3.3 lb)
- Oil for frying
- Salt, pepper
- Flour for frying
- Lemon wedges

Clean and wash the chicken and cut it into 8 - 10 pieces. Boil them in salted water for 10 minutes and drain them well. Mix the flour with the salt and pepper, dredge the chicken pieces in it and fry them in hot oil. Brown on both sides. Serve the chicken garnished with lemon wedges.

Kotopoulo Vrasto

Boiled Chicken

SERVES 6
- 1 large chicken about 2 kgs (4.4 lb)
- 1 large onion, sliced
- 2 stalks celery
- 2 carrots, sliced
- Whole peppercorns
- Salt
- 1 lemon, cut into quarters

Wash the chicken thoroughly. Place it in a large pot with the rest of the ingredients. Add water to cover and cook over medium heat for 1 1/2 - 2 hours. Remove the chicken and serve hot
Note: After straining the chicken broth, you may use it instead of water for boiling rice, or for making chicken soup.

Kotopoulo Lemonato

Chicken with Lemon

SERVES 4
- 1 medium-sized chicken
- 1/2 cup olive oil
- Salt, pepper
- Juice of 2 lemons

Wash the chicken and cut it into serving pieces. Heat the oil in a pot and sauté the chicken. Add the salt, pepper, lemon juice and 1 cup water and cook over low heat for about an hour. Serve the chicken with French fried potatoes or rice.

Kotopoulo Kokinisto

Chicken in Tomato Sauce

SERVES 4 - 5
- 1 chicken approximately 1 1/2 kg (3.3 lb)
- 1/2 cup olive oil
- 1 onion, finely chopped
- 1 tin chopped tomatoes
- Salt, pepper

Heat the oil in a pot and sauté the onion. Add the chicken, cut in serving pieces, and let it brown on all sides. Add the tomatoes, salt, pepper and 1/2 cup water and simmer for about an hour. Serve with French fried potatoes or rice.
Variations:1. If desired, sliced green peppers may be added along with the tomatoes.
2. For a lighter meal, the skin and fat may be removed from the chicken before cooking.

Agriogourouno Salmi

Wild Boar in Tomato Sauce

SERVES 8
- 2 kg (4.4 lb) wild boar meat
- 1/2 cup butter
- 6 ripe tomatoes
- 1 demitasse cup brandy
- Whole peppercorns
- A little flour or corn starch
- Salt, pepper

For the marinade:
- 3 cups red wine
- 2 carrots, sliced
- 2 onions, sliced
- 1 bay leaf
- Rosemary
- Thyme
- Whole peppercorns

Wash the meat, cut it into serving pieces and place it in an earthenware container. Pour the marinade over It and let it stand for two days, turning the meat from time to time to allow it to marinate thoroughly. Heat the butter and sauté the meat. Add a little of the liquid from the marinade, together with the vegetables, the tomatoes, peeled and put through a food mill, the salt and pepper, and cook slowly for 1 1/2 - 2 hours. Remove the meat from the pot and strain the sauce. Put it in a small pot and add the brandy. Mix a little flour in half a cup of water and add it to the sauce. Let the sauce boil a few minutes and pour it over the meat.

Stuffed Wild Duck

SERVES 4
- 1 wild duck
- 1/2 apple
- 1/2 cup olive oil

For the stuffing:
- 1 onion, finely chopped
- 300 gr (10.6 oz) sour apples, peeled and cut into cubes
- 1/2 tablespoon butter
- Celery, finely chopped
- 5 - 6 chestnuts, roasted and broken into pieces
- 1 small celeriac root

Pluck and singe the wild duck. Remove and discard the offal, reserving the liver. Wash the bird thoroughly and rub its body cavity with lemon, salt and pepper. Place the apple half and celeriac in the body cavity and sew it shut. Heat the oil in a pot, brown the duck , add a little water and let simmer until half cooked. Take the duck out of the pot, remove the apple and celeriac from the body cavity and reserve the juice. Blanch the liver, chop it fine, add it to the stuffing ingredients and mix. Stuff the duck and sew the body cavity shut. Baste with butter and place in a roasting pan together with some of the reserved juice. Roast in a moderate to hot oven for about an hour, basting from time to time with the pan juices.

Turtle Doves with Rice

SERVES 4
- 4 turtle doves
- 1/2 cup olive oil
- 2 medium onions, finely chopped
- 1 wineglass white unresinated wine
- 6 ripe tomatoes
- 1 clove garlic, finely chopped
- 1 green pepper, finely chopped
- 1 tablespoon butter
- 2 cups rice
- Salt, pepper

Pluck, singe and wash the turtle doves. Heat the oil and brown the birds with the onions. Add the wine, the tomatoes, peeled and put through a food mill, the garlic, green pepper, salt, pepper and a few tablespoons of water, and let the doves simmer until they are tender. Place them on a platter with half their juice and keep them hot. Put the rest of the juice, the butter, 4 cups water and a little salt into a small pot. Bring to a boil and add the rice. Reduce the heat, cover the pot and let simmer for 18 - 20 minutes. Put the rice on the platter with the birds and serve.

Rabbit Stew with Tiny Onions

SERVES 6 - 8
- 1 medium-sized rabbit
- 1 cup olive oil
- 1 large onion, finely chopped
- 1 wineglass dry red wine
- 4 ripe tomatoes or 1 tin peeled tomatoes
- 2 bay leaves
- 2 - 3 whole cloves
- Allspice
- 1 clove garlic
- 1 kg (2.2 lb) tiny onions
- Salt, pepper

Wash the rabbit thoroughly and cut it into serving pieces. Heat the oil, sauté the onion and rabbit and add the wine. Next add the tomatoes, peeled and put through a food mill, 1 cup water, the bay leaves, cloves, allspice, garlic, salt and pepper. Cover the pot and let the rabbit simmer over low heat for one hour. Clean and wash the tiny onions and cut a small cross in their root ends. Put the onions in the pot with the rabbit and continue to cook for about an hour.

Hare Stew with Tiny Onions

SERVES 6 - 8
- 1 medium-sized hare
- 1 cup olive oil
- 1 large onion, finely chopped
- 5-6 ripe tomatoes0
- 1 clove garlic, mashed
- 1 kg (2.2 lb) tiny onions
- Salt, pepper
- Vinegar
- 5-6 ripe tomatoes

For the marinade:
- 4 tablespoons olive oil
- 1 carrot, finely chopped
- 2 medium onions, sliced
- 1 stalk celery, finely chopped
- 2 bay leaves
- 2 whole cloves
- Pinch of thyme
- 1 clove garlic
- A few peppercorns
- 2 wineglasses dry red wine
- 4 tablespoons vinegar

Cut the hare into serving pieces. Wash it well in vinegar and water. Place it in an earthenware baking dish. Mix the marinade ingredients together and pour them over the hare pieces. Let the hare marinate in the refrigerator for 1 - 2 days. Drain the hare pieces and sauté them in hot oil, together with the onion. Strain the marinade, and add it to the pot along with the tomatoes, peeled and put through a food mill, the garlic, salt and pepper. Cover the pot and cook slowly for one hour. Peel and wash the onions and cut a small cross in their root ends. Put them in the pot with the hare and continue to cook over low heat for another hour.

Kouneli Kokinisto

Rabbit in Tomato Sauce

SERVES 6
- 1 medium-sized rabbit
- 1 cup olive oil
- 2 - 3 cloves garlic, finely chopped
- 6 ripe tomatoes
- Oregano
- Salt, pepper
- Pinch of sugar

Wash the rabbit and cut it into serving pieces. Heat the oil and sauté the rabbit. Add the garlic, the tomatoes, peeled and put through a food mill and the rest of the ingredients. Cook over low heat for about 1 1/2 hours.

Kouneli Gemisto Lemonato

Stuffed Rabbit with Lemon, a Specialty of Crete

SERVES 6
- 1 medium-sized rabbit
- 1 tablespoon butter
- 150 gr (5.3 oz) feta cheese, broken in pieces
- 100 gr (3.5 oz) walnuts, coarsely chopped
- 2 tablespoons crumbs of crustless bread
- 2 cloves garlic, finely chopped
- Parsley, finely chopped
- Juice of 2 large lemons
- Oregano
- 1/2 cup olive oil

Wash the rabbit, slit its belly open and remove the liver. Wash the body cavity thoroughly, salt it and rub it with a little butter. Blanch the liver and chop it fine. Add the feta cheese, the walnuts, the breadcrumbs, garlic, parsley, salt and pepper. Stuff the body cavity with the mixture and sew it shut. Heat the butter in a pot and brown the rabbit. Add a little water, cover the pot and cook slowly for about 1 1/2 hours. A few minutes before removing it from the heat, add the lemon juice and oregano. Let it boil for a few more minutes and serve.

Ortikia Pilafi

Quail with Rice

SERVES 4
- 4 large quail
- 2 tablespoons butter or margarine
- 1 wineglass white unresinated wine
- 4 ripe tomatoes
- 2 cups rice
- Salt, pepper

Pluck, singe and wash the quail, and rub them with salt and pepper. Heat the butter in a pot and brown the quail. Add the wine, the tomatoes, peeled and put through a food mill, and a little water. Cover the pot and cook slowly over low heat for approximately 40 minutes. Add 4 - 5 cups water. Increase the heat and when the water boils add the rice. Cover the pot and simmer for another 18 - 20 minutes.

147

MEAT-MINCED MEAT

Arnaki Exohiko

Lamb Country-Style

SERVES 6
- 1 kg (2.2 lb) leg of lamb
- 2 onions, finely chopped
- 1 cup butter
- 200 gr (7 oz) kefalotiri or kefalograviera cheese, broken into small pieces
- Salt, pepper
- 6 sheets of phyllo dough

Cut the meat into serving pieces and wash it. Cook the onion in a frying pan with a little water until it is soft. Add one teaspoon butter and sauté lightly. Add the meat, salt, and pepper and continue to sauté for a few minutes longer. Remove the pan from the heat, add the cheese and divide the mixture into portions. Brush the dough with melted butter, one sheet at a time. Place one portion of the meat mixture on each sheet and fold it into a rectangular packet. Place the packets in a greased baking pan, pour the remaining butter over them, and bake in a moderate oven for about one hour.

Moshari Stifado

Veal Stew with Tiny Onions

SERVES 5 - 6
- 1 kg (2.2 lb) shoulder of veal (without bones)
- 1 medium onion, finely chopped
- 1 cup dry red wine
- 1 cup olive oil
- 4 ripe tomatoes
- 1tablespoon tomato paste
- 1 bay leaf
- Salt
- Whole peppercorns
- 1 kg (2.2 lb) tiny onions

Wash the meat and cut it into serving pieces. Heat the oil and sauté the meat. Add the onion and continue cooking. Next add the wine, the tomatoes, peeled and put through a food mill, the tomato paste mixed in a cup of water, the bay leaf, the salt, the pepper and about 1 1/2 cups hot water. Cover the pot and let the meat simmer for 1 1/2 hours. Peel the onions and cut a small cross in their bases. Put the onions in the pot and continue cooking for an hour longer.

Hirines Brizoles Krassates

Pork Chops with Wine

SERVES 4
- 4 pork chops
- 1 small glass white unresinated wine
- 1/2 cup olive oil
- Salt, pepper

Wash the chops. Heat the oil and fry the chops on both sides. Add the wine, salt and pepper, cover the frying pan and simmer over very low heat until most of the liquid has evaporated, and only the oil is left.

Arnaki Souvlas

Spit-Roasted Lamb

- 1 lamb, 8-9 kg (17.6-19.8 lb)
- Butter
- Olive oil
- 2 - 3 lemons
- Salt, pepper

Remove the lambs' entrails including the larynx and large intestine, leaving the kidneys in place. Wash the lamb well and season the body cavity with salt and pepper. Skewer it carefully, from back to front. Fasten the backbone, neck and legs to the skewer with wire. Sew the belly shut. Rub the lamb all over with lemon juice, salt and pepper. Place it over the coals, which have been allowed to burn down. Turn the spit fast in the beginning and more slowly as the lamb cooks, until the skin is nice browned and it is done inside. As the lamb roasts, baste it with a mixture of melted butter and lemon juice.

Baked Lamb with Manestra

SERVES 5
- 1 kg (2.2 lb) lamb
- 1/2 cup butter or margarine
- 1 onion, finely chopped
- 4 - 5 ripe tomatoes
- 500 gr (17.6 oz) manestra (rice-like pasta)
- Salt, pepper
- Pinch of sugar
- Grated cheese

Cut the lamb into pieces and sauté it in the butter. Add the onion and continue cooking. Peel the tomatoes, put them through a food mill and put them into the pot, along with the sugar, salt, and pepper. Cover the pot and let the lamb cook slowly for about one hour. Put the lamb and its sauce in an earthenware baking dish (youvetsi) or a baking pan, and add the manestra and hot water (3 cups of water for each cup of manestra). Stir well, sprinkle with grated cheese and bake in a moderate oven for 30 - 40 minutes.

Lamb with Artichokes

SERVES 5
- 1 kg (2.2 lb) shoulder or saddle of lamb
- 8 spring onions
- 1/2 cup butter
- 2 carrots, thinly sliced
- 5 artichokes
- 1 lemon
- Fresh dillweed, finely chopped
- Salt, pepper
- Egg and lemon sauce (see Sauces)

Wash the meat and cut it into serving pieces. Heat the butter, sauté the meat and season it with a sprinkling of salt and pepper. Add a little water and let the meat simmer for one hour. Put a little water into a pot, add the onion and let it cook until the water has evaporated. Remove the stems, leaves and fuzz from the artichokes, cut them in half and rub them with lemon juice. Add the artichokes, carrots, dillweed and onions to the meat and continue to cook for another 30 minutes. Prepare the egg and lemon sauce, pour it over the meat mixture and serve.

Baked Lamb with Manestra ➡
Lamb with Artichokes ➡

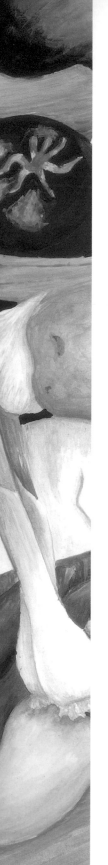

Stewed Lamb with Rice

SERVES 5
- 1 kg (2.2 lb) lamb shoulder
- 1/2 cup butter or margarine
- 1 onion, finely chopped
- 4 ripe tomatoes
- 2 cups rice
- Salt, pepper

Wash the lamb and cut it into serving pieces. Melt the butter and sauté the lamb pieces. Add the onion and continue cooking. Next add the tomatoes, which have been peeled and put through a food mill, the salt and the pepper. Cover the pot and let the lamb simmer for about one hour. Add 4 more cups of hot water and as soon as it comes to a boil add the rice and simmer for 18 - 20 minutes.

Arnaki Gemisto

Stuffed Lamb

- 1 small lamb, about 5 kg (11 lb)
- 1 set lamb offal (liver, heart, lungs, spleen, kidneys, sweetbreads)
- 1 bunch spring onions
- Fresh dillweed, finely chopped
- Fresh mint, finely chopped
- Feta cheese, not too salty, broken in pieces
- 3 cups rusk crumbs
- 5 tablespoons butter
- Lemon
- Salt, pepper

Remove the head from the lamb. Wash the body, season with salt and pepper, and rub it inside and out with lemon juice and butter. Bring the offal to a boil in a pot of water, drain it and cut it into small dice. Melt 2 tablespoons of butter and sauté the onions. Add the offal, the dillweed, the mint, salt and pepper and continue to sauté for a few minutes. Remove from the heat and stir in the cheese and rusk crumbs. Stuff the lamb and sew it shut. Put it in a roasting pan with a little water and roast it in a moderate oven for about 4 hours, basting it with its own juice from time to time.

Arnaki Lemonato

Lamb with Lemon

SERVES 6 - 8
- 1 1/2 kg (3.3 lb) leg of lamb
- 2 - 3 tablespoons butter
- Juice of 2 lemons
- 1 kg (2.2 lb) potatoes
- Olive oil for frying
- Salt, pepper

Wash the lamb, cut it into serving pieces and season it with salt and pepper. Heat the butter, brown the meat, add the lemon juice and a little water and let the lamb simmer for about 1 1/2 hours. Peel and slice the potatoes, salt them and fry them lightly. Just before the meat is done, add the potatoes, cover the pot and continue to cook until the lamb is tender and the potatoes are done.

Arnaki me Kolokithakia

Lamb with Courgettes (Zucchini Squash)

SERVES 6 - 8
- 1 1/2 kg (3.3 lb) loin of lamb
- 4 - 5 tablespoons flour
- 4 tablespoons butter
- 1 onion, finely chopped
- 4 - 5 ripe tomatoes
- Parsley, finely chopped
- Salt, pepper
- 1 kg (2.2 lb) courgettes (zucchini squash)

Wash the meat and cut it into serving pieces. Mix the flour with the salt and pepper and dredge the lamb pieces in it. Heat half the butter and sauté the lamb pieces with the onion. Add the tomatoes, which have been peeled and put through a food mill, the parsley and some water. Cover the pot and let the meat simmer for about an hour. Wash the courgettes and, unless they are tiny ones, cut them into small pieces. Heat the rest of the butter in a large frying pan and sauté the courgettes. Add them to the meat, cover the pot, shake it a few times and continue to cook for another 20-30 minutes.

Variation: Add salt and pepper to the courgettes as they sauté.

Fricassee of Lamb with Lettuce

SERVES 5
- 1 kg (2.2 lb) shoulder or saddle of lamb
- 1/2 kg (17.6 oz) spring onions, finely chopped
- 2 - 3 Romaine or Cos lettuces, thinly sliced
- 1/2 cup butter or oil or margarine
- Egg and lemon sauce (see Sauces)

Cut the lamb into serving pieces. Heat the butter or oil in a pot and sauté the meat. Add salt, pepper, the onions, lettuces, and a small amount of water. Cover the pot and let the fricassee simmer for about an hour. Prepare the egg and lemon sauce (with a little flour), pour it over the fricassee and serve.

Variations: 1. The onions can also be sautéed, but this makes the fricassee heavier.
2. Add finely chopped fresh dillweed.

Sofrito - a Specialty of Corfu

SERVES 6
- 1 1/2 kg (3.3 lb) leg of veal (without bone)
- 4 - 5 tablespoons flour
- 1/2 cup olive oil
- 4- 5 tablespoons vinegar
- 3 cloves garlic, crushed
- Parsley, finely chopped
- Salt, pepper

Mix the flour with the salt and pepper. Cut the meat into slices and dredge it in the flour. Heat the oil in a frying pan and brown the meat. Transfer the meat to a pot. Put the vinegar, the garlic, the parsley and a little water into the frying pan. When this sauce has come to a boil, pour it over the meat. Cover the pot and simmer for 1 1/2 - 2 hours.

Lamb Ragout

SERVES 6
- 1 1/2 kg (3.3 lb) leg or shoulder of lamb
- 1 onion, finely chopped
- 3 tablespoons butter
- 4 - 5 ripe tomatoes
- Dash of cinnamon
- Pinch of sugar
- Salt, pepper

Wash the lamb and cut it into serving pieces. Heat the butter and brown the meat with the onion. Add the tomatoes, after peeling them, removing their seeds and putting them through a food mill. Add the cinnamon, sugar, salt, pepper and a little water, and cook slowly for about 1 1/2 hours.

Lamb Offal Wrapped in Intestines

SERVES 4
- 1 set of lamb offal (liver, heart, lungs)
- Small intestines
- Sweetbreads
- 6 - 8 spring onions, finely chopped
- Fresh dillweed, finely chopped
- Parsley, finely chopped
- 3/4 cup olive oil
- Salt, pepper

Wash the intestines well, inside and out, and cut them into rather long pieces. Cut the offal into strips. Wrap up various pieces of the offal in the pieces of intestine. Put these into a roasting pan, add the onions, parsley and dillweed and sprinkle with salt and pepper. Pour the olive oil and a little water over the gardoumbes and roast them in a moderate oven, turning them from time to time until they are browned on all sides.

Oven - Roasted Lambs' Heads

SERVES 2
- 2 lambs' heads split in half
- 1/2 cup melted butter or margarine
- Salt, pepper
- Lemon juice

Wash the heads, rub them with lemon juice and season them with salt and pepper. Put them in to a roasting pan, cheek sides down. Pour the butter or margarine over them and roast them in a moderate oven, basting them from time to time with their own juices

Splinadero

Stuffed Large Intestine of Mutton

- 1 large intestine of lamb
- 1 set of mutton offal (excluding the lungs)
- Oregano
- 2-3 cloves garlic, finely chopped
- 50 gr (1.8 oz) kefalotiri cheese, cubed

Wash the intestine well, turning it inside out. Wash the offal, cut it into small pieces and sprinkle them with oregano, salt and pepper. Mix the offal with the garlic and cheese cubes. Stuff the intestine with the mixture and roast it on a spit over charcoal or in a moderate oven for 1 1/2 hours.

Note: If it is roasted in the oven, it should be basted with a little olive oil.

Bouti Arniou sto Harti

Roast Leg of Lamb in Paper

SERVES 6
- 1 leg of lamb, 1 1/2 kg (3.3 lb)
- 3 - 4 cloves garlic, sliced
- 2 tablespoons butter
- Salt, pepper
- 2 - 3 sheets of waxed paper

Wash the meat and cut slots in several places with the point of a knife. Insert a little butter and a sliver of garlic, dredged in salt and pepper into each slot. Season the joint with salt and pepper, rub it with butter and wrap it in the waxed paper. Tie it tightly with twine and roast it in a moderate oven for approximately two hours.

Arnaki Fournou

Oven-Roasted Lamb

SERVES 5
- 1 leg of lamb, 2 kg (4.4 lb)
- 2 - 3 cloves garlic, sliced
- Butter or margarine or olive oil, or butter and olive oil
- Juice of 1 - 2 lemons
- Thyme
- Salt, pepper
- 1 kg (2.2 lb) potatoes

Wash the meat. Make slits in several places with the point of a knife and insert slivers of garlic, seasoned with salt and pepper. Rub the joint with butter and place it in a roasting pan. Peel the potatoes, cut them into quarters and wash them. Sprinkle them with salt, pepper and thyme. Put them in to the pan with the meat and pour the oil over them, or dot with small pieces of butter. Add the lemon juice. Roast the lamb with the potatoes in a moderate oven for two hours

Sikoti Mosharissio Tiganito

Fried Veal Liver

SERVES 5
- 1 kg (2.2 lb) veal liver
- Flour
- Olive oil for frying
- Salt, pepper
- Lemon wedges

Wash the liver and slice it. Mix the salt and pepper with the flour. Dredge the liver in it and fry. Serve the liver garnished with lemon wedges.

Sikoti Arnissio Ladorigani

Lamb Liver with Olive Oil and Oregano

SERVES 4
- 1 kg (2.2 lb) lamb liver
- 1/2 cup olive oil
- Juice of one lemon
- Oregano
- Salt, pepper
- 1 bay leaf

Wash the liver, blanch, drain and cut it into small pieces. Place it in a pot, add the remaining ingredients together with a little water, and stir well. Let the liver simmer until it is done and of the liquid only the oil remains.

Beef Stew with Tiny Onions

SERVES 5 - 6
- 1 kg (2.2 lb) chuck or shin of beef
- 3 - 4 tablespoons flour
- 1/2 cup olive oil
- 1/2 cup red wine
- 2 cloves garlic
- Bay leaves
- 1 kg (2.2 lb) tiny onions
- 2 - 3 pieces of cinnamon bark
- 2 - 3 cloves
- 1 tablespoon tomato paste
- Salt, pepper

Cut the meat into large cubes. Mix the salt and pepper with the flour and dredge the meat in it. Heat the oil, sauté the meat and add the wine. Add the garlic, the bay leaves and three cups of hot water. Cover the pot and let the meat simmer until it is tender. Peel the onions and cut a small cross in the root end of each one. Add the onions, the cinnamon and the cloves, along with the tomato paste mixed with 1/2 cup hot water. Continue cooking for an hour longer.
Note: The onions may be sautéed in butter before being added to the meat.

The Drinker's Appetiser

SERVES 6 - 8
- 2 kg (4.4 lb) leg of veal (lean)
- 2 - 3 tablespoons butter
- 2 - 3 medium onions, finely chopped
- 2 - 3 cups dry red wine
- 2 cloves of garlic, crushed
- 1 bay leaf
- Whole peppercorns
- Cinnamon
- Allspice
- Oregano
- 1 tablespoon tomato paste
- 3 - 4 ripe tomatoes or 1 small tin tomatoes
- Parsley, finely chopped
- Salt, pepper

Wash the meat and cut it into large cubes. Heat the butter and brown the onion. Add the meat and spices and continue cooking. Add the wine, and then the tomato paste, the tomatoes and the parsley. Cover the pot and simmer for about 1 1/2 hours.
Note: If the sauce is too thin, add a little flour mixed with wine.

Moshari me Araka

Veal with Peas

SERVES 6

- 1 kg (2.2 lb) of veal shoulder (without bones)
- 2 - 3 tablespoons flour
- 2 medium onions, finely chopped
- 2 medium carrots, grated
- 1/2 cup white unresinated wine
- 1 bay leaf
- 4 - 5 ripe tomatoes
- 2 - 3 sprigs of parsley
- Bay leaf
- 500 gr (17.6 oz) cooked peas
- Salt, pepper

Mix the salt and pepper with the flour. Wash the meat, cut it into small pieces and dredge it in the flour.

Heat the butter and brown the meat. Add the onions and the carrots and continue to sauté.

Add the wine first, and then the tomatoes, peeled and put through a food mill, the parsley, the bay leaf, the salt and pepper and a good amount of water. Simmer the meat for about 1 1/2 hours. Add the peas and continue to cook for 10 minutes longer.

Moshari me Kolokithakia

Veal with Courgettes (Zucchini Squash)

SERVES 5 - 6

- Basic recipe Veal with Peas
- 1 kg (2.2 lb) small courgettes
- 2 tablespoons butter
- Salt, pepper

Prepare the veal as in Veal with Peas. Simmer the meat in its sause for 1 1/2 hours. Heat the butter in a large frying pan and sauté the courgettes. Add them to the meat in the pot and continue cooking for 20 - 30 minutes.

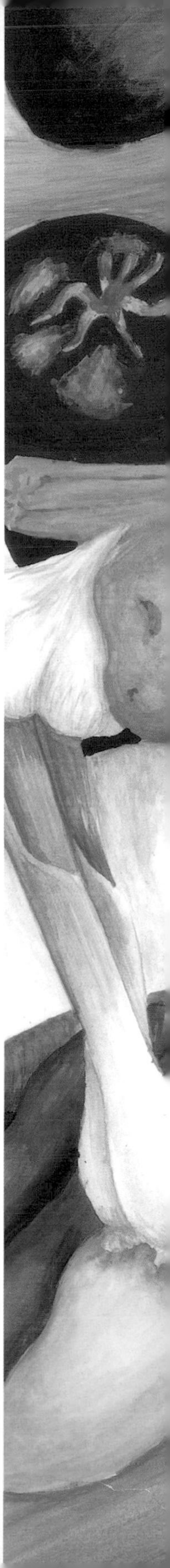

Hirino me Fassolia

Pork with White Beans

SERVES 8 - 10
- 500 gr (17.6 oz) dried white beans
- 2 kg (4.4 lb) boneless pork
- 1/2 cup olive oil
- 2 medium onions, finely chopped
- 1 glass of tomato juice
- 1 - 2 stalks of celery
- Red pepper
- Salt, black pepper

The evening before cooking, put the beans in water to soak. Next morning, drain the beans and boil them until partially cooked. Wash the meat and cut it into serving pieces. Heat the oil and brown the meat with the onion. Add the tomato juice, celery, salt, black and red pepper, and let the meat cook for about 1 1/2 hours until tender. Add the beans and a little hot water and continue to boil for half an hour longer.

Paidakia Arnissia Scharas

Grilled Lamb Chops

SERVES 4
- 1 1/2 kg (3.3 lb) lamb chops
- Oregano
- Salt, pepper
- 1/2 cup olive oil
- Lemon wedges

Wash the chops. Sprinkle oregano, salt and pepper over them. Brush them with olive oil and broil them under a hot grill. Serve garnished with lemon wedges.

Katsiki Riganato

Kid (Young Goat) in Oregano

SERVES 6
- 1 1/2 kg (3.3 lb) kid (front end)
- 3- 4 cloves garlic, halved
- 1 cup olive oil
- Oregano
- Salt, pepper

Wash the meat and cut slots in several places with the point of a knife. Put half a clove of garlic, dredged in salt and pepper, into each slot. Season the meat with salt and pepper, place it in a roasting pan, pour the oil and a little water over it, sprinkle it with oregano and roast it in a slow to moderate oven for 2 - 2 1/2 hours.

Pork with White Beans ➡
Grilled Lamb Chops ➡
Kid with Oregano ➡

Stuffed Kid

SERVES 6 - 8
- 1/2 kid (front half)
- 1 set offal
- 1 cup olive oil
- 500 gr (17.6 oz) spring onions, finely chopped
- Dillweed, finely chopped
- 1 - 2 ripe tomatoes

Blanch the offal, drain it and cut it into fine dice. Heat a little olive oil and sauté the offal, the onions and the dillweed. Add the tomatoes, peeled and chopped, the salt and pepper, and let the mixture cook until most of the liquid has evaporated. Wash the meat, season with salt and pepper, place the stuffing in the body cavity and sew it shut. Heat the rest of the olive oil in a large pot and brown the meat on all sides. Add a little water, cover the pot and cook over low heat until most of the liquid has evaporated and only the oil is left.

Pork with Celeriac

SERVES 5
- 1 kg (2.2 lb) pork shoulder
- 2 tablespoons butter
- 2 tablespoons flour
- 1 cup white unresinated wine
- 1 kg (2.2 lb) celeriac
- Egg and lemon sauce (see Sauces)

Wash the meat and cut it into serving pieces. Heat the butter, brown the meat and sprinkle it with flour. Continue to sauté for a few minutes and then add 2 - 3 cups hot water and the wine. Cover the pot and let the meat simmer for an hour. Clean the celeriac and cut it into pieces. Blanch and drain the celeriac pieces and add them to the meat. Continue to cook for about 30 minutes. Prepare the egg and lemon sauce, pour it over the entrée and serve.

Hirino Bouti Psito

Roast Leg of Pork

SERVES 8
- 2 kg (4,4 lb) leg of pork
- 1/2 cup olive oil
- Salt, pepper

Wash the meat, season it with salt and pepper and rub it with oil. Place it in a roasting pan, add a little water and cover with aluminium foil. Roast the joint in a moderate oven for 2 1/2 hours.

Moshari Kokinisto me Poure Melitzanas

Veal in Tomato Sauce with Aubergine Purée (A Specialty of Asia Minort

SERVES 5 - 6
- 1 1/2 kg (3.3 lb) rump of veal
- 2 medium onions, finely chopped
- 6 ripe tomatoes
- 2 kg (4.4,lb) aubergines (large purple type)
- 2 tablespoons butter
- Pinch of sugar
- 2 cups Bechamel sauce (see sauces)
- Salt, pepper
- Grated Parmesan cheese

Wash the meat and cut it into serving pieces. Heat the butter the sauté the meat with the onions. Add the tomatoes, peeled and chopped, the sugar, salt, pepper and a little water. Let the meat simmer for about 2 hours. Bake the aubergines in the oven, peel and purée them. Add the Bechamel sause and mix well. Serve the meat with the aubergine purée, sprinkled liberally with Parmesan cheese.

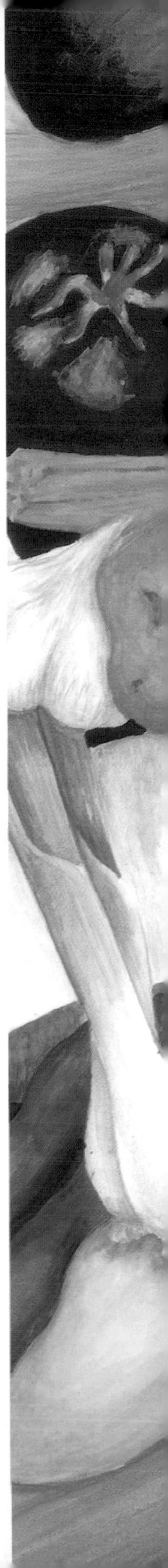

Lamb Offal on a Spit

- 1 set lamb offal (liver, heart, lungs, fat, sweetbreads)
- Small intestines of lamb
- 2 - 3 cloves garlic, crushed
- Parsley, finely chopped
- Salt, pepper
- Oregano

Wash the intestines well under running water, turning them inside out. Cut the offal into small pieces. Mix the parsley with the garlic, salt, pepper and oregano. Take each piece of offal, dip it into the seasoning and skewer it, alternating heart, lung, liver, etc. Wrap the whole spit with the intestines. Cook over hot coals for 1 1/2 hours, rotating the spit quickly in the beginning, and more slowly as the kokoretsi cooks.

Meat on a Spit

- 2 kg (4.4 lb) lamb or pork
- 3 - 4 onions, grated
- Salt, pepper
- Oregano

The day before cooking, wash the meat and cut it into small pieces. Spread the meat on a piece of waxed pepper and sprinkle it with oregano, salt and pepper. Add the onion, mix well and wrap the mixture up tight in the waxed paper. Leave it in the refrigerator for one day. The next day, skewer the meat on a small spit and roast it over a charcoal fire. Start out with the spit well above the fire, and lower it gradually as the meat cooks.

Lamb in Tomato Sauce

SERVES 5 - 6
- 1 1/2 kg (3.3 lb) shoulder of lamb
- 2 - 3 tablespoons butter
- 2 - 3 medium onions, finely chopped
- 1 small glass white wine
- 6 ripe tomatoes
- Salt, pepper

Remove the bones from the meat and cut it into small pieces. Heat the butter and sauté the meat. Add the onions and continue to sauté. Sprinkle with salt and pepper and add the wine. Peel the tomatoes, put them through a food mill and add them to the meat. Cover the pot and let the meat simmer for about an hour.

Jellied Pork

SERVES 8 - 10
- 2 kg (4.4 lb) leg of pork
- 5 carrots
- 1 onion
- Bay leaves
- 2 stalks of celery
- 4 hard boiled eggs
- Pickled cucumbers
- Allspice
- Salt
- Whole peppercorns

Wash the joint, put it in a pot and cover it with water. Bring to a boil, skim off the foam and add the salt, pepper and allspice. Reduce the heat and let the meat simmer for an hour. Add the carrots, onion, bay leaves and celery. Continue to cook over low heat for 2 hours longer.
Remove the meat from the pot and cut it into small pieces. Slice the eggs, carrots and pickled cucumbers, and arrange them in the bottom of a mold. Put the meat on top of them. Strain the liquid in which the meat was boiled and pour it into the mold.
Refrigerate until set.

Kelaidi

Garlicked Veal with Green Peppers, A Specialty of Larissa

SERVES 6 - 8

- 1 1/2 kg (3.3 lb) veal shoulder
- 500 gr (17.6 oz) green peppers
- 4 ripe tomatoes
- 1 whole bulb of garlic
- 250 gr (8.8 oz) feta cheese
- 250 gr (8.8 oz) melted butter
- Salt, pepper

Cut the meat, peppers, tomatoes and feta cheese into pieces. Put the meat in to an earthenware baking dish, followed by a layer of peppers and a layer of tomato slices. Add the garlic, finely chopped, and the cheese, pour the melted butter over the dish, and sprinkle with salt and pepper. Bake in a slow oven until the meat is tender.

Podarakia Arnissia Avgolemono

Lambs' Feet with Egg and Lemon Sauce

SERVES 6

- 2 kg (4.4 lb) lambs' feet, cleaned
- 1 - 2 stalks of celery
- 1 carrot
- 1 medium onion
- 1 bay leaf
- Whole peppercorns
- Salt
- Egg and Lemon Sauce (see Sauces)

Wash, blanch and drain the feet. Rinse them and place them in a pot. Cover with water and bring to the boil. Skim off the foam, add the vegetables, the bay leaf, the salt and pepper and cook over low heat. When the feet are done, remove them from the pot, take out the bones and cut them into pieces. Strain the liquid and return it to the pot with the feet. Prepare the egg and lemon sauce, pour it into the pot and serve.

Grilled Meatballs

SERVES 6
- 1 kg (2.2 lb) minced meat
- 1 cup rusk crumbs
- 1 egg
- 1 medium onion
- Parsley, finely chopped
- 1 tablespoon lemon juice
- Salt, pepper
- A little olive oil

Mix all the ingredients together, shape them into round patties about 1.5 cm (0.6 inches) thick, brush them with a little oil and cook them under the grill

Souvlakia Hirino i Mosharissio

Veal or Pork Shish Kebabs

SERVES 5
- 1 kg (2.2 lb) lean veal or pork
- 1/2 cup olive oil
- Oregano
- Salt, pepper
- Paprika
- 3 green peppers
- 3 tomatoes
- 4 medium onions

Cut the meat into cubes. Place them in an earthenware or glass bowl and add the remaining ingredients, except the vegetables. Let the meat marinate for 3 - 4 hours. Cut the vegetables into uniform pieces. Skewer the meat, alternating with a different vegetable each time. Grill the kebabs over charcoal, basting them from time to time with the marinade.

Veal with Macaroni

SERVES 6
- 1 kg (2.2 lb) veal shoulder (boneless)
- 2/3 tablespoons butter
- 4 ripe tomatoes
- 500 gr (17.6 oz) macaroni
- Salt, pepper
- Pinch of sugar
- Grated cheese

Wash the meat, cut it into small pieces and sprinkle salt and pepper over it. Heat the butter and sauté the meat until it has browned on all sides. Add the tomatoes, peeled and put through a food mill, a little more salt and pepper, the sugar and a little water, and allow the meat to simmer for 1 1/2 hours.

Add as much water as is needed to boil the macaroni. When it comes to a boil, add the macaroni, stir, cover the pot, reduce the heat once more and continue simmering until the macaroni is cooked Serve with grated cheese.

Note: As the macaroni cooks, stir from time to time and add more hot water if needed.

Moshari Lemonato

Veal with Lemon

SERVES 5
- 1 kg (2.2 lb) round of veal
- 2 tablespoons butter
- 1 bay leaf
- Juice of 1 lemon
- Salt, pepper
- Flour

Wash the meat and tie it. Heat the butter and brown the meat on all sides. Add a little water, the salt, pepper and bay leaf. Put the lid on the pot and let the meat simmer for about 2 hours. Mix a little flour in the lemon juice, add a little juice from the meat, mix well and pour over the meat. Let it cook a little while longer and serve.

Moshari Kokinisto

Veal in Tomato Sauce

SERVES 6
- 1 1/2 kg (3.3 lb) shoulder of veal
- 150 gr (5.3 oz) butter and olive oil
- 1 small glass dry red wine
- 2 pieces of stick cinnamon
- 5 - 6 ripe tomatoes
- Salt, pepper

Wash the meat and cut it into serving pieces. Heat the butter and oil and brown the meat on all sides. Add the wine, followed by the tomatoes, peeled and put through a food mill, the salt, pepper, cinnamon and a little water. Cover the pot and let the meat simmer for about 2 hours, adding water as necessary.

Miala Pane

Breaded Brains

SERVES 6
- 6 veal or beef brains
- Juice of 1 lemon
- 2 eggs, beaten
- 250 gr (8.8 oz) rusk crumbs
- 250 gr (8.8 oz) butter or margarine
- Salt

Wash the brains and put them in a pot. Cover with salted water and let them stand for 20 minutes. Remove the outer membrane and place the brains in boiling water to which the lemon juice has been added. Let them simmer for 20 minutes, drain them and cut them into slices. Dip each slice first into the beaten egg and then into the rusk crumbs. Heat the butter and fry the brains.

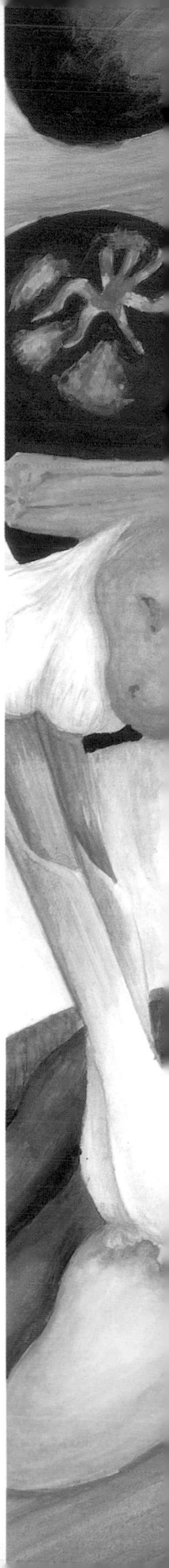

Brizoles Mosharissies Scharas

Grilled Veal Chops

SERVES 4
- 4 veal chops
- Olive oil
- Salt, pepper
- Lemon wedges

Wash the chops, brush them with oil, season with salt and pepper and cook them under a hot grill. Serve the chops garnished with lemon wedges.

Vodino Vrasto

Boiled Beef

SERVES 6
- 1 1/2 kg (3.3 lb) brisket of beef
- 1 onion
- 2 stalks celery
- 4 - 5 small carrots
- 3 leeks
- Bay leaves
- Whole peppercorns
- Salt
- 500 gr (17.6 oz) small potatoes

Wash the meat well. Peel and wash the vegetables. Bring a large pot of water to the boil and add the meat. Simmer for one hour. Then add the carrots, the leeks cut into large pieces, the celery, onion, bay leaves, salt and pepper, and continue to simmer for an hour longer. Add the potatoes and cook for another half hour.

Moshari me Melitzanes

Veal with Aubergines (Eggplant)

SERVES 5 - 6
- 1 kg (2.2 lb) rump or leg of veal (without bone)
- 50 gr (1.8 oz) butter
- 2 medium onions, sliced
- 5 - 6 ripe tomatoes
- 1 clove garlic, finely chopped
- 1 1/2 kg (3.3 lb) aubergines (long, narrow type)
- Olive oil for frying
- Salt, pepper

Wash the meat and cut it into serving pieces. Heat the butter and sauté the meat with the onion. Add the tomatoes, peeled and put through a food mill, the garlic, the salt, pepper and a little water and let the meat simmer for about 2 hours. Cut the aubergines into thick slices and fry them in plenty of hot olive oil. Add them to the meat and continue to cook for a few minutes before serving.

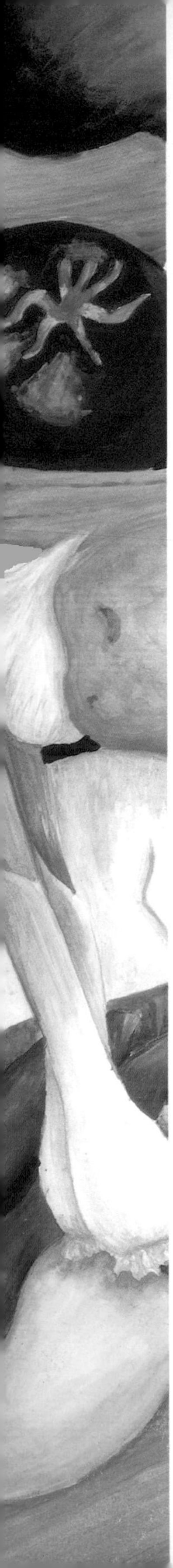

Horiatika Loukanika Tiganita

Fried Village Sausages

SERVES 6
- 6 village-made sausages
- Olive oil for frying
- Lemon juice

Cut the sausages into thick slices. Fry them on all sides in hot oil. Sprinkle them with lemon juice and serve.

Soutzoukakia Smyrneika

Smyrna Meat Rolls

SERVES 4
- 500 gr (17.6 oz) minced meat
- 1 cup stale crustless bread
- Cumin
- Salt, pepper
- 4 ripe tomatoes
- 2 cloves of garlic, crushed
- Pinch of sugar
- Olive oil for frying

Soak the bread and squeeze out all excess water. Mix the meat with the bread, garlic, cumin, salt and pepper. Knead the mixture and shape it into short sausage-shaped rolls. Fry them in the oil. Strain the oil and reserve about 1/2 cup. Put into a clean frying pan the tomatoes, which have been peeled and put through a food mill. Add the sugar, season lightly with salt and pepper and let the sauce simmer for about 10 minutes. Add the meat rolls and cook a short while longer before serving

Fried Meatballs

SERVES 6 - 8
- 500 gr (17.6 oz) minced beef
- 500 gr (17.6 oz) minced pork
- 250 gr (8.8 oz) bread (crust removed)
- 2 medium onions, finely chopped
- 2 eggs, beaten
- Mint, finely chopped
- Oregano
- Salt, pepper
- Flour
- Olive oil for frying

Soak the bread and squeeze out all excess water. Mix the meat, bread, onion, eggs, mint, oregano, salt and pepper. Knead the mixture well and shape it into patties. Dredge them in flour and fry them in plenty of hot oil.

Meatballs in Tomato Sauce

SERVES 6 - 8
- Fried Meatballs (see recipe above)
- 4 ripe tomatoes
- 1 tablespoon tomato paste
- 2 tablespoons olive oil
- 1 bay leaf
- Pinch of sugar
- Salt, pepper

Peel the tomatoes and put them through a food mill. Place them in a pot with a little water and all the other ingredients, except the meatballs, and simmer for 20 minutes. Add the meatballs, cook for a few minutes longer and serve.

Splina Gemisti

Stuffed Spleen

SERVES 4
- 1 large veal spleen
- 200 gr (7 oz) feta cheese, broken into pieces
- 1/2 cup rusk crumbs
- 3 cloves of garlic, finely chopped
- Parsley, finely chopped
- 4 ripe tomatoes
- 1 cup olive oil
- Salt, pepper

Score the spleen and slit it lengthwise. Mix together the feta cheese, the rusk crumbs, garlic, parsley and a little olive oil. Season the mixture with salt and pepper, stuff the spleen and sew the opening shut. Place it in a roasting pan, and pour the olive oil and the tomatoes, which have been peeled and put through a food mill, over it. Cook the spleen in a moderate oven for about 50 minutes.

Moshari me Bamies

Veal with Okra

SERVES 5 - 6
- 1 kg (2.2 lb) shoulder of veal (bones removed)
- 1 kg (2.2 lb) okra
- 1 wineglass vinegar
- 3/4 cup olive oil
- 5 - 6 ripe tomatoes
- 1 onion, finely chopped
- Salt, pepper

Wash and clean the okra, mix it well with the vinegar and salt and let it stand for half an hour. Wash the meat and cut it into serving pieces. Heat the olive oil and brown the meat on all sides. Add the onion and continue to sauté. Add the tomatoes, which have been peeled and put through a food mill, together with the salt, pepper and a little water. Cover the pot and let the meat simmer for 1 to 1 1/2 hours. Rinse the okra well and put it into the pot with the meat, adding a little water if necessary. Cover the pot, give it a couple of shakes and simmer for 40 minutes.

SWEETS

Baklavas

- 500 gr (17.6 oz) phyllo dough
- 800 gr (1 3/4 lb) almond meats, coarsely chopped
- 2 teaspoons cinnamon
- Pinch of ground cloves
- 1 cup butter
- 2 cups sugar
- 1 cup honey
- Juice of 1 lemon
- 2 teaspoons vanilla

Mix the almond meats with the cinnamon and cloves. Butter a baking pan and line it with 4 phyllo sheets, brushing each one with melted butter. Sprinkle on a little of the filling, add two more buttered sheets of dough, and continue in the same way, leaving 4 sheets of dough for the last layer. Cut into diamond-shaped pieces, down to the bottom of the baklava. Pour the rest of the butter over the top and bake in a moderate oven for 40 - 45 minutes.Place the sugar, honey, 1 1/2 cups water, the vanilla and the lemon juice in a pan and boil for 5 - 6 minutes. Skim off any foam that forms and pour the hot syrup over the lukewarm baklava.Serve cold. **Variation**: 400 gr walnut meats may be substituted for half the almond meats.

Galaktomboureko

Milk Pie with Syrup

- 120 gr (4.2 oz) semolina
- 1 kg (2.2 lb) sugar
- 4 eggs
- 1 kg (2.2 lb) hot milk
- Grated orange rind
- 250 gr (8.8 oz) butter
- A few drops lemon juice
- 500 gr (17.6 oz) phyllo dough

Beat together the semolina, 300 gr (10.6 oz) of the sugar and the eggs. Put the mixture in a pot, add the milk little by little, heat and boil for a few minutes. Add the orange rind.
Line a baking pan with half the phyllo dough, brushing each sheet with melted butter. Let the sheets of dough hang out a few inches over the sides of the pan. Pour in the filling and fold the overhanging sheets over the top. Place the remaining phyllo dough on top of the pie, buttering as before. Bake in a moderate oven for 1/2 hour. In the meantime, prepare the syrup by boiling the rest of the sugar in 250 gr (8.8 oz) water, to which the lemon juice has been added, for 5 minutes. Pour the syrup over the baked milk pie.

Karidopita

Walnut Cake

- 2 tablespoons butter
- 2 cups sugar
- 2 eggs
- 1/2 cup milk
- 1 cup ground walnuts
- Sprinkling of cinnamon
- 1/2 teaspoon ground cloves
- 2 tablespoons brandy
- 4 cups flour
- 1 tablespoon rusk crumbs
- 3 tablespoons baking powder
- Juice of 1/2 lemon

Cream the butter. Beat in the eggs, alternating with 1/2 cup of the sugar. Add the milk, walnuts, cloves, cinnamon, brandy and finally the flour, which has been sifted together with the baking powder. Butter a baking pan and sprinkle the rusk crumbs in the bottom. Pour in the batter and bake for an hour in a moderate oven. Boil the rest of the sugar in 2 cups water, to which the lemon juice has been added, for five minutes, and pour the syrup over the walnut cake.

Keik Sokolatas

Chocolate Cake

- 1/2 cup butter
- 1 1/2 cups sugar
- 2 eggs
- 50 gr (1.8 oz) melted baking chocolate
- 1 cup evaporated milk
- 2 cups flour
- 1 level tablespoon baking powder
- A little butter for the cake pan
- A little flour for the cake pan

Cream the butter and sugar. Add the eggs, one at a time, beating constantly. Add the baking chocolate, and then alternate the flour, mixed with the baking powder and the milk, continuing to beat.
Butter and flour a cake pan and pour in the batter. Bake the cake in a moderate oven for 40 minutes.

Keik me Yaourti

Yoghurt Cake

- 1 1/2 cups sugar
- 1 cup butter or margarine
- 4 eggs
- 1 small container yoghurt
- 3 cups flour
- 1 level tablespoon baking powder
- A little butter to grease the cake pan

Cream the sugar and butter. Add the eggs. one at time, beating constantly. While still beating, add the yoghurt and the flour, mixed with the baking powder. Beat the batter thorougly. Butter cake pan and pour the batter in. Bake in a moderate oven for 1/2 hour.

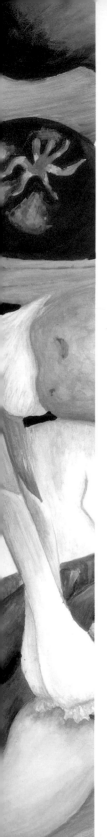

Yoghurt Cake with Syrup

- 1 cup butter
- 4 cups sugar
- Grated orange rind
- 1 teaspoon vanilla
- 4 eggs
- 1 small container of yoghurt
- 3 cups flour
- 1 tablespoon baking powder
- 2 tablespoons brandy
- 40 gr (1.4 oz) almonds, blanched and chopped

Shift the flour with the baking powder. Cream the butter with half the sugar. Add the vanilla, grated orange rind and the eggs, one at a time, beating constantly. While continuing to beat, add the flour and baking powder, alternating with the yoghurt. Finally, add the brandy and beat the batter until it is smooth.

Butter a small baking pan, pour in the batter and sprinkle the almonds over the top. Bake the yoghurt cake in a moderate oven for approximately 50 minutes.

When the cake has cooled, boil the rest of the sugar with 1 cup water for 5 minutes. Pour the hot syrup over the cake.

Honey Puffs

- 25 gr (0.9 oz) yeast
- 500 gr (17.6 oz) flour
- 1 level teaspoon salt
- Olive oil for frying
- Honey
- Cinnamon
- Coarsely ground walnuts (optional)

Dissolve the yeast in 1/2 cup lukewarm water. Mix the flour with the salt in a deep bowl. Make a well in the middle of the flour and pour in the yeast and water. Gradually add another cup of lukewarm water, stirring the mixture until it becomes a uniform, rather thick batter. Cover and leave it in a warm place for about 1 1/2 hours, until bubbles rise to the top. Heat the oil. Using a wet teaspoon, take spoonfuls of the batter and drop them into the hot oil. Continue until there is no more batter left. Turn the puffs with a slotted spoon until they are golden brown all over. Pour honey over them and sprinkle them with cinnamon and coarsely ground walnuts.

Yoghurt Cake with Syrup ➡
Honey Puffs ➡
Apple Pie ➡

Apple Pie

- 3 cups flour
- 1 level teaspoon salt
- 3/4 cup margarine
- 2 tablespoons rusk crumbs
- 1 kg (2.2 lb) sour apples, grated
- 1/2 cup sugar
- 1 tablespoon lemon juice
- 1/2 cup walnut meats, finely chopped
- Sprinkling of cinnamon
- 1 egg white

Shift the flour together with the salt. Add the margarine, cut into small pieces. Rub in the margarine and add 3-4 tablespoons of cold water. Knead the dough lightly and divide it into two parts. Roll out half the dough and line a pie pan with it, sprinkling the rusk crumbs over the bottom. Mix the rest of the ingredients, except the egg white, and fill the crust. Roll out the rest of the dough, cover the pie with the top crust, prick it in several places with a fork, and brush it with the lightly beaten egg white. Bake the apple pie in a moderate oven for 50-60 minutes.

Pear Compote

- 1 kg (2.2 lb) pears
- Lemon juice
- 2 cups sugar
- 2 whole cloves
- 1 piece stick cinnamon

Peel the pears, cut them in half and remove the seeds. Place them in a pot with two cups of water and the juice of one lemon. Add the remaining ingredients and boil the pears until they are soft. Serve cold.

Oil Cake

- 5 eggs
- 2 cups sugar
- 1 cup sunflower oil
- 2 1/2 cups flour
- 1 tablespoon baking powder
- 1 cup orange juice
- Grated orange rind
- Oil for the cake pan
- A little flour for the cake pan

Beat the eggs and sugar well. Add the oil, continuing to beat. Mix the flour with the baking powder and add it to the mixture, alternating with the orange juice. Add the grated orange rind and continue to beat. Oil a cake pan lightly and flour it. Pour the batter in and bake in a moderate oven for 40 minutes.

Fanouropita

St. Fanourios' Yeast Cake

- 3 cups flour
- 1 cup sugar
- 1 1/2 teaspoons cinnamon
- 1/2 cup sunflower oil
- 1/2 tablespoon ouzo or mastic brandy
- 2 eggs
- A little grated mastic
- 10 gr (0.4 oz) yeast
- 1/2 cup raisins
- A little oil for the pan
- A little flour for the pan

Dissolve the yeast in tepid water. Mix together all the ingredients, including the yeast, and knead. If the dough is too stiff, add a little water. Oil and flour a baking pan. Place the dough in it and cover it with aluminium foil. Put the pan on top of a pot of boiling water until the dough has risen. Remove the aluminium foil and bake in a moderate oven for 40-45 minutes.

Damaskina Komposta

Prune Compote

- 500 gr (17.6 oz) dried prunes
- 1/2 cup sugar
- 2- 3 whole cloves
- 1 piece stick cinnamon
- A few drops of brandy

Put the prunes in water to soak the evening before cooking. Next morning, wash them and put them in a pot with 1 1/2 cups water, the sugar, cloves and cinnamon. Boil the prunes until they are soft and add a few drops of brandy. Serve cold.

Komposta me Xera Frouta

Dried Fruit Compote

- 500 gr (17.6 oz) various dried fruit (prunes, figs, apricots, raisins, etc.)
- 4 level tablespoons sugar
- 50 gr (1.8 oz) blanched almonds

Wash the fruit and soak it for a few hours until it is soft. Place it in a pan with 1 cup water and the sugar. Boil for 15-20 minutes. Serve the compote chilled, garnished with the almonds.

Halvas with Semolina

- 4 cups sugar
- 1 kg (2.2 lb) water
- 1 cup olive oil or butter
- 50 gr (1.8 oz) coarse semolina
- 1/2 cup blanched almonds, halved
- Sprinkling of cinnamon

Boil the water with the sugar for about 10 minutes, or until the syrup has thickened slightly. Heat the oil or butter, add the semolina and stir until it is golden brown. Add the syrup, continuing to stir until the mixture is thick. Stir in the almonds, and remove the pot from the heat. Put the halvas in a mold, and when it has cooled turn it out on a platter and sprinkle it with cinnamon.

Mila Psita

Baked Apples

- 8 large red apples
- 9 tablespoons sugar
- 2 tablespoons brandy
- 1 tablespoon lemon juice
- 2 - 2 tablespoons butter
- Blanched almonds, broken in pieces.

Peel the apples and use a corer to remove the cores. Wash them and place them in a pot. Put a tablespoonful of sugar in the cavity of each one. Add 1/2 cup water, the brandy and the lemon juice, and boil for 20 minutes. Place the apples in a baking dish and pour the liquid from the pot over them. Put a little butter and a few almonds in each apple. Bake them in a hot oven for a few minutes until they are golden brown.

Moustalevria

Must Pudding

- 1 kg (2.2 lb) must (unfermented wine)
- 250 gr (8.8 oz) semolina
- 1 cup coarsely ground walnuts
- Cinnamon
- Sesame seeds

Place the must and the semolina in a pan and bring to a boil over medium heat, stirring constantly until thick. Serve the must pudding in small bowls with ground walnuts, sesame seeds and cinnamon sprinkled over the top. Serve cold.

Halvas with Semolina ➡
Baked Apples ➡
Must Pudding ➡

Crullers

- 4 cups self-raising flour
- 4 tablespoons sugar
- 4 eggs
- Grated lemon rind
- 2 tablespoons olive oil
- Olive oil for frying
- 2 cups honey
- Cinnamon
- Coarsely chopped walnuts

Put the flour in a deep bowl. Make a well in the middle of the flour and pour in the well-beaten eggs, the sugar, lemon rind and oil. Knead well to form a stiff dough. Divide the dough into equal parts and roll it out in thin sheets. Cut each sheet into strips.

Heat the oil well and drop in the strips of dough. Twist them around to form circles in the oil and fry them until they are golden brown.

Boil the honey with 1 cup sugar. Skim off the foam, pour the syrup over the crullers and sprinkle them with cinnamon and walnuts.

Semolina Cake

- 1 cup butter
- 4 cups sugar
- 6 egg yolks
- 6 egg whites
- Grated orange rind
- 1 cup flour
- 2 cups fine semolina
- 1 tablespoon baking powder
- Juice of 1/2 lemon

Cream the butter with 1/2 cup sugar. Add the yolks, one at a time, together with the orange rind, beating constantly. Add the flour and baking powder, alternating with the milk, stirring all the time. Add the semolina, and finally fold in the stiffly beaten egg whites. Butter a baking pan and pour the batter into it. Bake in a moderate oven for 40 minutes.

In the meantime, prepare the syrup. Boil the rest of the sugar in 1 1/2 cups of water, to which the lemon juice has been added, for five minutes. Pour the syrup over the cake, while it is still hot.

Cream Kadaifi

- 450 gr (15.8 oz) sugar
- 2 eggs
- 200 gr (7 oz) flour
- 500 gr (17.6 oz) milk
- A little vanilla
- 200 gr (7 oz) butter
- 200 gr (7 oz) kadaifi pastry
- 600 gr (1 1/3 lb) whipped cream

Mix the sugar, eggs and flour together in a pot. Add the milk, little by little, heat and boil for a few minutes, stirring constantly. Remove from the heat and add the vanilla and a little butter.Line a buttered baking pan with the kadaifi pastry and bake it in a moderate oven until it is golden brown. Prepare the syrup by boiling 150 gr (5.3 oz) sugar in 75 gr (2.7 oz) water. Pour it over the baked kadaifi. Pour the milk mixture over the top and refrigerate. Before serving, garnish the kadaifi with whipped cream piped on in parallel lines.

Kadaifi Yannina-Style

- 1 cup walnut meats, finely chopped
- Sprinkling of cinnamon
- 500 gr (16.7 oz) kadaifi pastry, combed out
- 250 gr (8.8 oz) phyllo dough
- 4 cups sugar
- 1 cup butter
- 1 slice lemon

Butter half the phyllo sheets and use them to line a buttered rectangular baking pan. Place half the kadaifi pastry on them and sprinkle the walnut meats and cinnamon over it. Add another layer of kadaifi pastry and finally the remaining buttered phyllo sheets. Pour the remaining melted butter over the top and score the top few phyllo sheets in strips lengthwise. Bake the kadaifi in a moderate oven for approximately 1 hour. In a pan, boil the sugar in 2 1/2 cups of water with the lemon slice for 5 - 10 minutes until thickened. Let the syrup stand until lukewarm, and pour it over the kadaifi.
Variation: Almonds may be substituted for the walnuts.

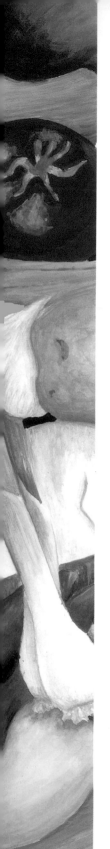

Halvas, Farsala-Style

- 250 gr (8.8 oz) rice flour
- 500 gr (17.6 oz) sugar
- 3/4 cup butter
- 1/2 cup blanched almonds

Dissolve the rice flour in 2 cups water. Boil the sugar in 1 cup water and cook it until it has caramelised and is a rich brown colour. Reduce the heat and add 3 cups hot water, the rice flour and the butter, stirring constantly with a wooden spoon. Let the mixture cook over medium heat until it has thickened, stirring all the time. When it has browned on the bottom and is thick, pour it into a baking pan and sprinkle the surface with sugar.

Greek Doughnuts

- 2 cups water
- 1/2 cup butter
- Pinch of salt
- ! cup durum wheat flour
- 3 eggs
- Olive oil for frying
- Cinnamon
- Honey

Put the water, butter and salt on to boil in a pot. When it come to the boil, add the flour, stirring vigorously until the mixture is thick. Let it cool a few minutes and add the eggs one by one, beating constantly until the butter is smooth. Heat the oil and drop spoonful of the batter into it. Fry them uniformly over medium heat until they are golden brown. Pour honey over them, sprinkle with cinnamon and serve.

Fried Phyllo Dough Sticks

- 500 gr (17.6 oz) phyllo dough
- 500 gr (17.6 oz) sugar
- Olive oil for frying
- Sprinkling of cinnamon

Separate the phyllo sheets. Wrap them one by one around a wooden dowel 1/2 inch in diameter. Pull out the dowel to form thin tubes of dough. Cover them with a damp towel to keep them from drying out. Boil the sugar with a cup of water for 2 minutes. Cut the phyllo tubes into inch-long pieces and fry them in hot oil. Pour the syrup over them immediately and sprinkle them with cinnamon.

Krema Vanila

Vanilla Pudding

- 4 eggs
- 5 level tablespoons sugar
- Pinch of salt
- A few drops of vanilla
- 3 cups hot milk
- 1 1/2 teaspoons butter

Beat the eggs together with the sugar, salt and vanilla. Add the milk a little at a time, beating constantly. Pour the mixture into a small pan and place it in a larger pan of slowly boiling water. Stir continually until the pudding has thickened. Remove it from the heat, add the butter and stir. Served chilled.

Krema Sokolata

Chocolate Pudding

- 5 tablespoons corn starch
- 3 cups milk
- 1 cup sugar
- 5 tablespoons cocoa powder
- Vanilla

Put the corn starch, the sugar and 1/2 cup of the milk in a small pan. Place it in a larger pan of slowly boiling water. Heat the rest of the milk and gradually add it to the mixture, stirring constantly. Add the cocoa and the vanilla, stirring all the time, until the cocoa has dissolved and the pudding is thick. Serve hot or cold.

Rizogalo

Rice Pudding

- 1/2 cup sugar
- Cinnamon
- Vanilla
- 4 tablespoons short-grain rice
- 4 cups hot milk
- 1 heaping tablespoon corn starch

Put the rice on to boil in 3/4 cup of water. Add 3 1/2 cups milk and continue to boil over low heat for approximately half an hour. Add the corn starch dissolved in the rest of the milk, along with the vanilla and the sugar. Simmer the rice pudding until it has thickened. Serve hot or cold, with a sprinkling of cinnamon.

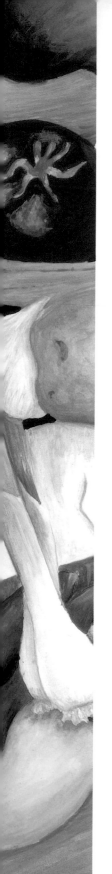

Sweet Easter Bread

- 50 gr (1.8 oz) yeast
- 1 cup evaporated milk, undiluted
- 1 cup sugar
- 1 teaspoon salt
- 250 gr (8.8 oz) butter
- 4 egg yolks
- 4 egg whites
- Grated lemon rind
- 1 kg (2.2 lb) flour
- A few blanched almonds, broken

Dissolve the yeast in 1/2 cup lukewarm water. Warm the milk and add the sugar, salt and butter. Beat together the yeast, egg yolks and lemon rind and add them to the milk. Add the flour, beating constantly. Knead the dough thoroughly, cover it and leave it in a warm place until it has doubled in size. This will take about 1 1/2 hours. Knead the dough again and shape it into Easter cakes. This is done by making 3 cylinders of dough about 2.5 cm (1 inch) thick and braiding them. Brush the cakes with the lightly beaten egg whites, sprinkle with almonds and bake them in a moderate oven for 20-30 minutes.

Koulourakia Smyrneika

Smyrna Cookies

- 1250 gr (2.8 lb) butter
- 1 kg (2.2 lb) powdered sugar
- 4 egg yolks
- 4 kg (8.8 lb) flour
- 2 tablespoons baking powder
- 2 teaspoons baking soda
- 1/2 cup orange juice
- 2/3 cup brandy
- Vanilla
- 1 beaten egg for glazing

Cream the butter with the sugar. Add the egg yolks one by one, beating constantly. Sift the flour with the baking powder and baking soda and add it to the mixture, little by little. Next, gradually add the orange juice and brandy, and finally the vanilla. Knead the ingredients together thoroughly and form into small circles or fancy shapes. Brush them with the beaten egg and bake in a moderate oven for about 20 minutes.

Sweet Easter Bread ➡
Smyrna Cookies ➡

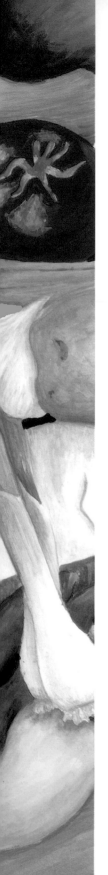

Koulourakia Paschalina
Easter Biscuits

- 1 kg (2.2 lb) flour
- 2 level teaspoons baking powder
- 1 teaspoon baking soda
- 2 cups butter
- 3 cups sugar
- 2 eggs
- A few drops of vanilla
- 5-6 tablespoons milk
- 1 beaten egg for glazing

Sift the flour with the baking powder and baking soda. Beat the eggs and vanilla into the butter. While still beating, add the flour little by little, alternating with the milk. Knead the dough well and form into small rings or fancy shapes. Place them on a buttered baking sheet and brush them with the beaten egg. Bake in a moderate oven for 15-20 minutes.

Koulourakia Nistissima
Lenten Cakes

- 1 1/2 cups olive oil
- 2 cups sugar
- 1 1/2 cups orange juice
- 2 teaspoons baking soda
- 1 wineglass brandy
- 1250 gr (2.8 lb) flour
- Oil for the baking sheet

Beat the sugar into the olive oil. Add the orange juice, the baking soda, dissolved in the brandy, and finally the flour, little by little. Knead the ingredients together thoroughly. Form the dough into 6-inch (15 cm) long cylinders the thickness of a finger. Shape it into circles or twists or figure-eights, place them on a lightly oiled baking sheet and bake them in a moderate oven for about 20 minutes.

Amigdalota
Marzipan Pears

- 600 gr (21.1 oz) almond meats
- 1 1/2 cups sugar
- 1/2 cup rusk crumbs
- Powdered sugar
- Orange blossom water
- A few whole cloves

Blanch the almonds, slip off the skins and chop them fine in the blender. Add the sugar, rusk crumbs, a tablespoonful of orange blossom water and half a glass of water. Knead the mixture well and shape it into small pears, inserting a clove in the bottom of each one. Let them stand for a few hours. Rub a baking pan with butter and line it with waxed paper. Place the marzipan pears on it and bake them in a moderate oven for 20-25 minutes. When they are cool, sprinkle them with orange blossom water and roll them in powdered sugar.

Skaltsounia

Nut Pies

- **For the crust:**
- **300 gr (10.6 oz) flour**
- **1 tablespoon butter**
- **1/2 teaspoon baking soda**
- **Juice of 2 oranges**

- **For the filling:**
- **1 cup coarsely ground walnuts**
- **1 cup coarsely ground blanches almonds**
- **2 level tablespoons sugar**
- **Cinnamon**
- **1 tablespoon honey**

- **For the topping:**
- **Orange blossom water**
- **Powdered sugar**

Mix together the ingredients for the crust and knead well. Roll out the crust 1/2 inch (1.2 cm) thick and cut into 4 1/2inch rounds. Mix the filling ingredients together thoroughly and place a spoonful of filling in the centre of each dough round. Wet the edges with a little water and fold over into half-moon shapes. Bake in a slow oven for 35 minutes. When the pies are lukewarm, sprinkle them with orange blossom water and powdered sugar.

Kaltsounia

Sweet Cheese Dumplings, a Specialty of Crete

- **For the crust:**
- **1 cup butter**
- **1 cup sugar**
- **1 cup milk**
- **3 eggs**
- **2 teaspoons vanilla**
- **1 teaspoon bicarbonate of ammonia**
- **1 kg (2.2 lb) soft wheat flour, or enough to make a stiff dough**

- **For the filling:**
- **1 kg (2.2 lb) fresh mizithra cheese**
- **3 eggs**
- **1 cup sugar**
- **Cinnamon**
- **1 egg for glazing**

Cream the butter, eggs and sugar thoroughly. Add the flour little by little, alternating with the milk, and finally the vanilla and bicarbonate of ammonia. Knead together well. Roll out the dough 1/2 inch (1.2 cm) thick and cut out 4-inch (10.2 cm) rounds. Put the mizithra cheese through a food mill, add the rest of the filling ingredients and mix. Place a teaspoonful of the filling on each round of dough. Bring the dough up from 4 points to meet in the centre, forming square dumplings. Brush them with the beaten egg and bake them in a moderate oven for 30 minutes.

Honey Macaroons

- 1 1/2 cups olive oil
- 1 1/2 cups butter
- 1/2 cup sugar
- 1 1/2 cups orange juice
- 2 level teaspoons baking soda
- 1/2 cup brandy
- Grated orange rind
- About 1300 gr (2.9 lb) flour
- Walnuts, coarsely grated
- Cinnamon

For the syrup:
- 1 1/2 cups honey
- 1 1/2 cups water
- 1 1/2 cups sugar

Beat the olive oil, butter and sugar together thoroughly. Add the baking soda, dissolved in the orange juice, together with the brandy and the grated orange rind, continuing to beat. Finally, add flour little by little until a soft dough is formed. Knead the dough well and form it into ovals 2 1/2 inches (6.4 cm) long. Bake in a moderate oven for 25-30 minutes. Boil the syrup ingredients for 5 minutes. When the macaroons are partially cooled, pour the hot syrup over them. Sprinkle with walnuts and cinnamon.

Almond Shortcakes

- 500 gr (17.6 oz) fresh butter of the finest quality
- 150 gr (5.3 oz) sugar
- 2 egg yolks
- 250 gr (8.8 oz) toasted almonds, broken in pieces
- 2/3 cup brandy or orange juice
- A few drops of vanilla
- 1 kg (2.2 lb) flour
- 1 cup orange blossom water
- 300 gr powdered sugar

Cream the butter and sugar until light and fluffy. Add the egg yolks, the almonds, the brandy or orange juice and the vanilla, beating constantly. Add the flour little by little and knead all the ingredients together. Shape the dough into thick patties 1 1/2 - 2 inches (3.8 - 5 cm) in diameter, and bake in a moderate oven for 20 minutes. While still hot, sprinkle with orange blossom water and roll in powdered sugar.

Must Cakes

- 1 cup olive oil
- 1/2 cup petimezi (molasses-like syrup made from must, or unfermented wine)
- 1 heaping teaspoon bicarbonate of ammonia
- 1 cup must (unfermented wine)
- 1 level tablespoon powdered cloves
- 2 tablespoons brandy
- Juice of 1/2 lemon
- 4 cups flour
- A little oil for the baking sheet

Beat the oil into the petimezi. Add the bicarbonate of ammonia, dissolve in the must, along with the cloves, brandy and lemon juice. Beat well to mix. Add the flour little by little, mixing continually. Cover the dough and let it stand for 30 minutes. Form 6-inch (15 cm) long cylinders the thickness of a finger. Shape them into circles, place them on an oiled baking sheet, and bake them in a moderate oven for 20 minutes.

Honey Macaroons ➡
Almond Shortcakes ➡

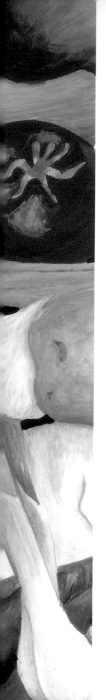

Vassilopita

New Year's Cake, a Specialty of Asia Minor

- 2 cups butter
- 2 cups sugar
- 1 cup milk
- 2 eggs, beaten
- 1 cup finely ground blanched almonds
- 1/2 cup brandy
- 1 kg flour
- 2 teaspoons baking powder

Mix the baking powder with the flour. Cream the butter and sugar. Add the rest of the ingredients and beat the batter until it is light and fluffy. Butter a baking pan and pour in the batter. Bake in a moderate oven for about 40 minutes.

Bougatsa

Milk Pie with Cinnamon

- 1 1/2 cups granulated sugar
- 3/4 cup fine semolina
- 3 eggs
- 6 cups hot milk
- Grated lemon rind
- 150 gr (5.3 oz) melted butter
- 500 gr (17.6 oz) phyllo dough
- Powdered sugar
- Cinnamon

Beat the semolina together with the granulated sugar and the eggs. Place the mixture in a pot and add the hot milk, little by little beating constantly. Bring to a boil for a few minutes. Finally add the grated lemon rind. Line a buttered baking pan with half the phyllo sheets, brushing each one with melted butter. Pour in the filling and cover with the remaining sheets, buttering as before. Bake the pie in a moderate oven for about 20 minutes. Before serving, sprinkle with powdered sugar and cinnamon.

Tiganites

Pancakes

- 250 gr (8.8 oz) flour
- 1 egg
- Pinch of salt
- 1/2 teaspoon oil
- 1 1/2 cup milk
- Olive oil for frying
- Honey
- Cinnamon

Place the flour with the salt in a deep bowl. Make a well in the centre of the flour and put in the egg and the oil into it. Mix together, adding the milk little by little. Drop spoonful of the batter into plenty of hot oil. Fry the pancakes until they are golden brown. Serve with honey and cinnamon.

S P O O N   S W E E T S

Vissino Gliko

Sour Cherry Preserves

- 1 kg (2.2 lb) sour cherries
- 1 kg (2.2 lb) sugar

Wash the cherries and remove the stems and pits. Place the pits in 2 cups of water; drain it off and put it in a pot, together with the cherries and sugar. Let stand to draw the juice out of the cherries. Boil for 10 minutes. Drain off the syrup and put it on to boil for 10 minutes longer, skimming off any foam that forms. Add the cherries and boil for 2-3 minutes longer. Remove the pot from the heat and when the sweet has cooled put it in glass jars.

Nerantzi Gliko

Bitter Orange Preserves

- 1 kg (2.2 lb) small green bitter oranges
- 750 gr (1.7 lb) sugar
- 200 gr (7 oz) glucose

Wash the oranges and remove the seeds with a nail or bamboo skewer. Place them in a pot, cover them with water and boil for 10 minutes. Drain off the water and put the oranges into cold water. Let them stand for 8 days, changing the water 2-3 times a day, until they have lost their bitterness. Boil the sugar for 5 minutes in 1 1/2 cups water. Add the oranges and boil for 10 minutes. Let them stand for 24 hours. Add the glucose and boil until the syrup is thick. Cool and store in glass jars.

Karidaki Gliko

Green Walnut Preserves

- 1 kg (2.2 lb) small unripe walnuts
- 2 kg (4.4 lb) sugar
- Stick cinnamon
- Whole cloves
- Vanilla

Punch a hole in each walnut with a large nail. Boil them until they are soft. Drain, cover with cold water and let stand for 3 days, changing the water often, until they are no longer bitter. Boil the sugar in 1 kg (2.2 lb) of water for 5 minutes. Add the walnuts and boil for a few minutes longer. Next day, bring the preserves to the boil again with a few whole cloves and piece of stick cinnamon and cook until the syrup has thickened. Cool and store in glass jars.

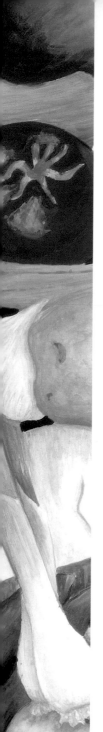

Stafili Gliko

Grape Preserves

- 1 kg (2.2 lb) seedless grapes
- 500 gr (17.6 lb) sugar
- 4 tablespoons orange juice
- Vanilla

Remove the stems from the grapes and wash them well. Place them in a pot with the sugar, the orange juice and 1/2 cup water and simmer for 10 minutes. Next day, bring them to the boil again and cook until the syrup is thick. Remove from the heat and add the vanilla. When they have cooled, store them in glass jars.

Sikalaki Gliko

Green Fig Preserves

- 1 kg (2.2 lb) small green figs
- 1 1/2 kg (3.3 lb) sugar
- 1/2 cup lemon juice

Punch a hole in each fig with a large nail. Boil them in plenty of water. Test them for doneness by removing one and pushing a toothpick down through the top. If it falls from the toothpick, it is done. Heat the sugar in 4 cups of water until bubbles begin to form. Add the figs and boil until the syrup is thick. Finally, add the lemon juice. Store the preserves in glass jars.

Milo Gliko

Apple Preserves

- 1 kg (2.2 lb) tiny apples (firikia)
- Juice of 2 lemons
- 1 kg (2.2 lb) sugar
- Vanilla
- Almonds, blanched and toasted

Peel and core the apples, using a corer. Wash them well and put them in water with the juice of 1 lemon. Boil 1 cup sugar in 2 1/2 cups water and a few drops of lemon juice for 5 minutes. Add the apples and the rest of the sugar and cook until the apples are rather soft. Let stand overnight. Next day, bring the preserves to the boil again to thicken the syrup. Shortly before removing them from the heat, add the vanilla and let cool. Place one almond in the cavity of each apple and store them in glass jars.

1. HARD CHEESES

GREEK GRAVIERA (GRUYERE)
An eating cheese with a pleasant taste and rich aroma.
CRETAN GRAVIERA
A choice eating cheese with a pleasantly sweetish taste and rich aroma.
KEFALOTIRI
A salty grating cheese with a pleasant sharp taste and rich aroma.
MYTILENE LADOTIRI
A hard cheese with a salty taste and a pleasant aroma.
BATZOS
Produced mainly in Central and Western Macedonia and Thessaly. A hard, salty cheese usually eaten cooked (in pizza, grilled or fried).
FORMAELLA PARNASSOU
A hard cheese. It has a pleasant taste and aroma, particularly when cooked.

2. SEMISOFT CHEESES

KASSERI
Mainly an eating cheese, made from sheep's milk or a mixture of sheep's and goat's milk; it has a pleasant taste and aroma.
SFELA
Produced in the southern Peloponnese. It is a semisoft, rather salty cheese, ripened and preserved in brine.

3. SOFT CHEESES

GALOTIRI
Produced in Epirus and Thessaly, it is a soft speadable eating cheese which forms the base for many appetisers.
KOPANISTI
Produced in the Cyclades, this creamy, salty cheese has a distinctive sharp taste.
TELEMES
Ripened and preserved in brine, it is a rich, soft, salty cheese with a slightly pungent taste.
FETA
Feta cheese is ripened and preserved in brine. It has a slightly pungent taste and a rich aroma.

4. WHEY CHEESES

ANTHOTIRO
A white eating cheese, ready to be eaten as soon as it is made. It may be kept for a few days in the refrigerator.
MANOURI
Manouri is produced in Central and Western Macedonia and Thessaly. It is a rich, soft eating cheese with a very pleasant taste.
MIZITHRA
A rich, soft eating cheese with a pleasant taste. It may be kept for a few days in the refrigerator.
Aged Mizithra, which has undergone a dehydration process, is used as a grating cheese for spaghetti, cheese pies, etc.
XINOMIZITHRA
A rich, soft cheese, usually salty, with a sharp taste and pleasant aroma.

Note: All cheese should preferably be kept refrigerated